Drawn by the talented Neve Clark.

Dedication

For my children, always shine your light into the world, do what makes you happy, be who you were meant to be and honour who you are, I love you forever.

For my husband thank you for always supporting me, and our family I love you with all that I am.

To all of you who will pick up this book, follow your dreams, be amazing!

"Thank you, for buying my story, what you need to know about me, I am not tech savvy, yet I've done this all by myself, and the experience I had trying to publish this book, well I could write a book about that! So, you may come across some grammar and punctuation errors thanks to the demons that live in my computer! The aim of this book is to encourage you to live your truth, so if you come across an error, smile, and think ah she's only human!"

Please note: All topics in this book are of my own personal experience, and actual events, I do not wish to offend or upset anyone with my experiences. This is a spiritual book and the experiences in here are personal to me and acquaintances who have given permission to be in this book. This book is about my own personal journey and awakening to the spirit world and the struggles I had understanding what everyone else seemed to do naturally. The aim of this book is to help people understand that it is ok to not progress as quickly as others, and that whether your spiritual or not, if you have a dream keep reaching for it until it is yours!

Contents.   *Page:*

Introduction

"From frustrations and a sense of not belonging, to seeing spirit but not understanding them, to becoming an animal communicator and a healer.

"A world so huge it will never be discovered."

A walk through my personal spiritual journey and the frustrations that came with it!

There have been 3 people on this journey,

Me, the eager dedicated go getter,

Myself, the doubt the low self-esteem and the negative version of me,

And spirit, the trustworthy silent advisor, who when you start to listen, will talk louder!

Welcome to my book, trust me when I say this, if you are reading this book then I truly hope you will feel better and less frustrated with your own personal path at the end of it!

This book is about my spiritual journey and the path that led me to it, not all is as it seems in this crazy unpredicted, experience that we call life!

I have 3 gorgeous girls, 2 dogs a guinea pig and a husband, that's enough about that for now let's see where all this fits in, as I take a walk back through my life with the help of my guides.

Let's get straight into why it is you've been drawn to my book!

Spirit!!! What does it mean to you? To me its love. Its universal love and energy, its where our souls go when we transition and if we are lucky enough, we can connect with them even when they've crossed over.

But be prepared because it also brought me frustration, tantrums, tears, and self-doubt but this has never stopped me from trusting in them 100% I hope my journey into the life I now live can help you understand that all these feelings are normal and are a huge part of your growth and experience here on earth...

I wish I could say here is where it all started, when I first thought about writing this book, I thought I knew exactly when it started. The truth is, as I've been writing spirit have been sending me memories and important experiences, and I've now realized, I have always been on this journey, spirit have just been waiting for me to wake.

It has not been easy trust me. the ups the downs, the highs, and lows and then the tears and oh yes, tantrums of why this path was so hard for me, and so easy for others!

Then there's that word PATIENCE! if I never hear it again, it will be a blessing.

I hope this book will help you feel more at ease that what you may be experiencing is normal for you, there are a few words of wisdom from my guide White Eagle,

I could not have written this without the support of my spiritual team.

For any family and friends who have found this book,

I shelter you from this part of my world, because I understand it's not everyone's belief, I am proud of who I am and all those that I have helped by walking this path,

So, you're in for an eye-opening look into the world, my world, of Angels, healing, visitations, visions and my absolute pride and joy animal communication.

This is my story....

"Animals are the greatest Teachers, we could learn so much from them, if we just knew how to listen"

I sat up, and there sitting on the end of my bed was a young girl, long blonde hair wearing a pretty, pink dress,

My heart stopped beating and my body was frozen, and just like that she was gone!

Chapter 1

All about me!

I'm a normal mum of 3, my life is crazy busy, there has been troubles and miracles, like any normal person's life, the only difference is I felt my life was missing something. I felt different to others, the way I viewed the world was like I knew it before, before the hate, the cruelty, I just don't understand how people could cause pain to others, I used to listen to stories that my Gran told and they felt so familiar, and yet, I was jealous that the world I lived in was so far from what she remembered. I felt I was here to make a difference to teach, to share kindness, to help others.

Her words to me would be

"I dread the world your children are going to live in"

I didn't understand at the time as I was only young, but those words have stayed with me and now they make sense.

Life isn't bad though is it, where there is cruelty, there is double the kindness, where one family suffer a tragedy there are 10 families offering help.

I believe life is what we make of it, I have 3 beautiful daughters whose beauty shines the most from within, they are all so different but as equally kind as one another, Libbie is a beautiful soul she is so laid back, she would offer her last to you, I remember once she was about 5 years old Freya was new born, Neve was 8, and they had a pound pocket money off a relative, Neve lost hers in the car and was so flustered over it. Libbie said here you can have mine and Neve took it! this is a story that always makes me laugh and shows how different they are, I'm very proud of my children and the characters that they have, me and Libbie can laugh over something so stupid but actually split our sides over it, she has such a comical streak that she makes me laugh over things I probably shouldn't! She is the friend that is always there for everyone and will stand up for what she believes, she has a beautiful innocent heart that shines brightly to the world, my gran would say that girl lights up the room!

Neve shares my sense of humour or at least she gets it, she is my more anxious child, but is very self-aware, she is strict with her time and perfection is everything to her, Neve is currently in college doing graphic design, and is drawing some beautiful characters for a friends up-coming book! I'm so proud of the young lady she is, her heart is pure.

Then there is Freya hilarious and very kind this is a quality they all share. Freya can make your heart melt with kindness and innocence.

It hasn't always been easy, but it's always been entertaining, Freya was diagnosed with epilepsy at 9 months old which left her with global delayed development life was a challenge on times, she never slept, she was always on the go! Freya was my youngest and she is an absolute gift to the world we live in, everyone who meets her loves her, they talk about her and instantly get emotional, and this is Freya's gift, her purpose is to share kindness and love into the world, she was born on Saint David's day and really is a beautiful yellow daffodil bringing in upliftment to the lives she touches! We all have a gift and a purpose, some peoples purpose may not be obvious to you, as they may be of a low energy, but their purpose is to teach you.

When Freya was young, we would avoid all parties, weddings, and any huge social occasion, because people just didn't understand her needs, Freya had no understanding of danger, she didn't understand instructions, and could get a little aggressive in certain situations, if she got over excited, overt tired or hot she would have seizures, so it was easier and less stress for me as a mum to avoid all stressful occasions, but Andrew would take our other 2. Life can be hard so if there is a way, we can help to make it easier and avoid stressful situations we do it.

There was a section of my life which I know now was building my strength, building my resistance, testing me as a light worker,

It was back in 2014, the phone rang it was my mum, "dads taken Rhys to the hospital he can't walk!" Rhys is my brother he had been having pain in his neck and back and had these lumps, the doctors told him it's nothing to worry about! Anyway, long story short, it was non- Hodgkin's lymphoma, we were at the hospital when a brave, yet distraught Rhys asked, "am I going to survive this?" it was stage 4!

The doctor shrugged his shoulders and replied "I don't know" my poor parents were distraught, the whole of my body wanted to fall to the floor, but this strength came over me and I knew then someone had to hold it together. I wrapped my arms around Rhys and said, "you are going to beat this, you are going to fight, and we are going to help you!"

A few days had past, and I felt this overwhelming urge to visit the crematorium and talk to my Grampa, him and Rhys were so close I knew he would be watching over him! As we pulled up with some yellow carnations, I got out of the car and it hit me I had no idea what row he was in, I hadn't been there in a while and there were more rows added, with panic as the children and Andrew were in the car waiting I started to walk, I believed even then that family were watching over us and hearing our words and thoughts, so, I sent up a message, "please Grampa where are you" I walked past a few rows and then suddenly yet gently my body turned it was like I was in a trans, like I was just there and not even thinking, then I stopped I looked down and there he was Harry Prince. I put the flowers down and begged him to help my brother, I said I will do anything but please save him. With tears filling my eyes and a lump in my throat I walked back to the car.

It was a long few months Rhys had no movement in his legs and was told he would never walk again. This was hard to hear but I said, "as long as you're here it doesn't matter just remain positive," yes, I probably drove them nuts, because I was positive, I was trying to keep it light and keep them all uplifted, yet I'd get home and once the

*children were in bed I'd totally break down, I
wanted to go to the highest mountain and
scream! Scream all this anger and pain out from
my body, I needed to release.*

*A few weeks had passed Rhys was having all the
treatments that he needed,*

*The phone rings "guess what I'm doing?" Rhys
says,*

"what" I replied.

"I'm wiggling my big toe!"

*This was the best news yet! Rhys beat the cancer,
it wasn't easy he really suffered but he beat it, and
he is walking, running, swimming, and doing all
these amazing things.*

*The doctors said they have never seen anything
like it. I really believe positivity and determination
played a huge part in this!
Rhys recovered, and then came the diagnosis of
dementia with my beloved Mam, (Gran)*

We were taking it in shifts to stay with her, and around these shifts I was running back and for to hospital appointments with my daughters, Libbie was being assessed by education psychologist for dyslexia, Freya was under, occupational therapy, physiotherapy, speech and language and the neurologist, and Neve with severe anxiety, so to say I didn't have time to do anything else was an understatement! My house was an absolute tip! But I honestly did not care! It was so busy, and people needed me, so housework was last on the list, but one thing I always lived by was this,

"When things are ok even if it is that 10-minute cup of tea, embrace it, put your feet up and relax, let your mind switch off and just breath, let your energy rebalance".

This saved me, and I tell all my clients the same, when things are good, we are recharging so we can be ready for the next challenge, and for a month or so that's what I did, I'd get a phone call at least 3 times a week regarding Freya and incidents of falling, so when I would receive no bad news, I would celebrate that day! This is just a little of my crazy life, I was the entertainment for most people as they couldn't believe my luck or life, yes it was bloody hard, but it really showed me the strength I have! And really made me appreciate life and the little things. That is why we are given challenging experiences to find our inner strength or to change something that needs changing in our lives! We may not be aware that something in our life must change, but spirit is always aware and always have a plan so if you don't see the signs they will step in, and sometimes it takes something huge to get you to notice! just like my best friend Hayley.

Chapter 2

Do angels exist?

Yes!

Angels are a huge part of my life and journey, they deserve, respect and acknowledgment. Angels can come to you in any shape or form, just ask for them to help, Angels will not intervene unless they're called on, the more you ask and be open the more you will realise they have been there all along guiding you, supporting you holding you, If, your team of angels need to though they will find a way to step in and take control! I have had so many experiences with these beautiful angelic beings of light, I talk more about this through the book.

"Just because we can't see something,

Doesn't mean it doesn't exist!"

Here is a truly powerful story of betrayal, depression, hitting the lowest part of your life and a guardian angel!

My best friend Hayley and I have been inseparable since the age of 3, 2 little girls starting school together and what we didn't realise is 37 years later we would still be best friends!

Let's skip the next 34 and a half years as there's not enough trees in the world as it is!

Me and Hayley would speak every day, so when I couldn't get hold of her over the weekend I was concerned, I messaged her daughter who replied.

"she's still in hospital."

Me, "WHAT! WHAT HAPPENED"

Sophie always was a little to calm!

"Ah the dog bit her lol!" her actual response

What happened was so bad, her finger was amputated, and she endured hours of surgery,

Both hands were in plaster, and she had no use of them, so she relied on help off her partner of 23 years,

A few months passed, it was a Monday morning in September, and I had just dropped Freya off to school, when a text popped up,

"Can you ring me when you have 5, I need you" it was Hayley.

I phoned her right there, "what's happened?"

"he's left me, she sobbed he's been carrying on,"

I drove straight to her I couldn't go in as the 2 dogs were so aggressive, she was now a prisoner in her own home, so we went up to the top of a mountain where it was private,

I cannot go into the details as I need to protect her, but she told me that weekend he disappeared she was worried sick and didn't know what was happening, when he turned up, he said I'm leaving you! I've met someone,

Then she told me that she tried jumping in front of a train! And my world came crashing in on how serious this was, how could all this have happened over a weekend!

She said she just had no thoughts, no feelings, she just walked and didn't care, then this man came from nowhere and grabbed her he saved her! He then left his journey to accompany her home, this man was put there that day to save her, because this wasn't the end of Hayley's story, the next 2 years were so horrific, to watch your best friend go through a break down, anorexia and such low self-esteem, it was worrying and exhausting but I knew it was for a reason, I knew one day we would look back and say this had to happen, although at that time not even I knew the reason, I trusted in the universe and the powers it has. I knew something needed changing even if Hayley didn't, in January 2020, everything came to light for Hayley and at the same time the life she knew came crashing in on her like an avalanche of lies and betrayal, she was in work when the breakdown happened, and she's been home ever since, the stress caused her so much illness, but through it all we have managed to try and keep hopeful that it was all worth it!

Hayley met a lovely man named Wayne, and she now knows what happiness is, she knows what relationships are supposed to be like, we go out for meals as a double date something we have never been able to do, Hayley's previous relationship was not what it seemed, and nobody saw it, nobody but spirit, looking back there is still work to be done with her, and wounds that will never heal but she is loved now like she deserves to be, and she never thought that would be possible so I thank the gentleman on the platform that day, was he really an angel? no, he was sent to that spot at that time to save her, she never got his name, he was a true hero a silent hero sent by Hayley's guardian angel and I've no doubt that this changed the life path he too is on!

I talk about Hayley a bit later on, on how spirit use any open connection to pass on a message.

Chapter 3,

Anxiety comes knocking!

Everything I write about in this book is all connected to where I am today, Spirit is definitely bringing up these stories and helping me even now understand them and what their purpose was,

It was March 2015 and time for school, my eldest daughter Neve, was in comprehensive, and she was going to miss her bus, she kept complaining of feeling unwell so I contacted the school to tell them she would not be in, soon as the bus had gone, she made this miraculous recovery! This went on for 6 weeks, I finally had some help from school and the doctors who said this was in fact anxiety, and not a illness, they said it was all in her head, Well I know it's in her head that's a bit of a stupid thing to say to a parent whose daughter is worrying her so much I had to go on anti-depressants, Anxiety is a huge problem and there should be more help out there for people not the rubbish we had which was a few websites to visit!! I am not going into the extent of the anxiety out of respect for my daughter, but what happened next was quite amazing. I wasn't at all into spiritual things in fact I'd run a mile if something paranormal happened, I'm petrified of horror films but love medium and ghost whisperer and remember thinking how amazing this would be to help these people, I did however always look for the reason behind things, the silver lining and always tried to be positive, well back to Neve I remember one day, sifting through Facebook in a daze just trying to occupy my mind when an advert popped up this is what I saw.

ACHIEVE HYPNOSIS

Do you suffer with ANXIETY blah blah ANXIETY blah blah ANIXIETY blah blah ANXIETY blah blah ANXIETY......?
ANXIETY....... CHILD ANXIETY....

Get in touch with Andrea.

I messaged the lady a huge paragraph of how awful everything was and is there anything she could do because am desperate and Camhs (child and adolescent mental health service) couldn't help as the lady she was under, went on the sick with anxiety!

Anyway, the reply was "Hi Rhian I absolutely can help, and I will fit you in through my lunch break tomorrow,"

I went back to the advert, and it read.

Achieve Hypnosis

Do you struggle with weight loss, anxiety, phobias, or a fear of childbirth, why not try out hypnosis a proven alternative treatment to help retrain the brain on how it thinks of these things?

Message me for more information.

I was so confused? What happened all I saw was the words ANXIETY literally jumping out of the page! What I did not know was this was the start to my spiritual awakening!!!

We went to the hypnotherapy session, and it was amazing Andrea was so understanding, compassionate and reassuring, we had a few more sessions and Neve was back in school, the anxiety is still around but nothing to what it was like, I kept in touch with Andrea on and off about Neve what I did not know was the role she was going to play in my journey this will come later in the book….

I started down the route of craft, painting wooden objects, this really helped my mind to relax and rest away from the stress and worry of Neve, all I would think about was the next project. Do not get me wrong she was obviously on my mind constantly, but this was a great distraction. I made some beautiful creations and met a few new people one of which was Lisa known as the crystal lady! Lisa run's a beautiful business called the Crystal Haven, little did I know that Lisa was going to be a teacher of mine! Oh, how the sneaky universe works it's so clever and when I look back, I am in disbelief that my beautiful journey started because of such a worrying time in my life...

That is usually how it starts though for some; I thought my journey started when my beautiful gran passed away, but no it was a few years previously, slowly awakening to the wonders of this magnificent universe we live in.

Soon after Neve started back to school, I found myself waking at night with poems in my head I would write them down and go back to sleep. I would then wake with new ideas of things to make, memorial angels, moons etc. these sold well and with my own personal poetry on them. Little did I know I was being guided,

(I am telling you this as one day you will look back and see the journey and how it all connects to where you are now!)

One day I'm driving to my Grans, and I get this absolute energy come over me, that's it no more crafts I'm finished, it served its purpose, this was a huge shock because I absolutely loved making these creations, but every ounce of passion I had literally left me there on that round about.

I now know I needed the craft to go and make room for more important things like my Gran.

"Sometimes things appear in our lives to distract our minds from what does not serve us."

(WHITE EAGLE)

Chapter 4

My hero Mamgu.

(Gran)

It is early summer 2016, and I am driving to my grans and singing my head off to Titanium by Sia, which is my favourite song to release stress and tension, this is a regular thing now my poor mam has early onset dementia, but nobody wants to admit it yet as she is the glue to our family, my hero. My auntie and mum do a rotating night shift and I help in the day and a few hours in the evening bless her she cannot be left alone now so one of us is always there but that is ok we would do anything for her, she's one of the kindest most soulful people I've ever known and well I wouldn't be who I am without her. Leading up to her passing a year later was so hard, I remember on the last few days she was confusing day with night, telling us to be quiet and to turn the lights out at 2 p.m.! My mum said that her and auntie had been talking and said that it is getting to much and we may have to consider a home for her, but mam would get so stressed with change they said the only way we could do this is if she was in hospital. I went back up that night for a few hours and she slept quite a bit, my mum came to take over and as I left mam said to me "where are you going?" I said, "I'm going home now mam I've been here since 5, I need to put the girls to bed," which she replied "well I'm really going to miss you" at that moment my world came crashing in I looked at my mum and said this is it you know. I had to hold back the tears and lump in my throat while I replied, "I will miss you too." I gave her a kiss on the forehead holding back the tears and left. I cried all the way home!

That night she fell and was taken to hospital.

Mam was in for a few days and the doctor said this is the end of her journey, my mum was in disbelief, but the doctor was right, a few days passed, and she was very unwell, then came that moment of clarity I was waiting for, we were wheeling her bed into a private room when she grabbed my hand and said,

"Well, hello what are you doing here?"

I replied, "what do you mean I haven't left your side!" we had a brief conversation telling her we were staying with her and that was it she went into a state of unconsciousness, me my mum and auntie stayed there a few nights reminiscing laughing uncontrollably then crying uncontrollably, mam was unconscious and we were begging Grampa to come and take her, we were sat quietly exhausted and emotional and I was playing with her wedding ring on her finger thinking to myself I wish I could have this so you will always be with me, and that moment I felt a hand on my head! Nobody was behind me, and I knew it was her. She passed peacefully away with me, my mum and auntie around her holding her it was a gift that we could be with her, but it also totally broke our hearts,

I came home and slept, the next day I was sitting watching blankly at the tv, when I realized a song was playing in my head, the words were on repeat.

"Even if you cannot hear my voice, I am right beside you dear."

I knew instantly that this was mam! I felt tingles all over my head and face,

I visited the house every day asking her to come close but nothing I felt so sad, I was expecting to see her or hear her talk I did not understand how spirit worked, but I knew this wasn't the last I would see of her, I could feel it in me like she was there with me encouraging me, talking to me but I just couldn't hear or see her.

One day I was there with my mum and auntie, they said, "Rhian we were wondering if you'd like mams wedding ring?" I was so delighted, and it fitted perfectly mam must have heard me and made this happen...

The ring

A few of Mam's sayings were...

"Que sera, sera,"

"Smile and the world smiles with you."

I live my life with these sayings imbedded within me, because she was one incredible woman who I could not bear to be without so they took her bit by bit until we were all ready to let her go and for that I will always be grateful for...

Years earlier I had a dream, I was in an empty pool, then my Grampa appeared. I was so

excited to see him I was 9 when he died and stayed with mam on the weekends to keep her company, or talk her ears off, we grew so close she said I saved her, the truth was I didn't want to be anywhere else. He looked at me and said I've come to take mam it's her time! Oh my god I cried, and I begged him not to, I cried so much it woke me and I cried even more! So, I really believe mam went the way she did because any other way would have broken our hearts beyond repair, and my *personal path may have not been this way, so I truly thank spirit and my Grampa for that. Little did I know it wasn't a dream it was a visitation!*

Back to Mam.

Planning the funeral was so surreal, myself my mum, Auntie Cheryl and cousin Bethan would meet at mams, and plan, mam was 92 so there wasn't many people left of her friendship group to

invite, the songs were picked but we couldn't think of the perfect song for her to go out to, we thought and thought and I had this song constantly playing in my head since she past, it was driving me crazy because me and mam always watched the film, every night as she loved

Doris Day, Auntie said I don't want it to be sad I want it to celebrate her and that's when I said what about

"By the light of the silvery moon" perfect and it was decided, they asked me to write and read the eulogy and I couldn't have been prouder this was my chance to really do her proud, I believe she was there watching and shedding a few tears, but I got through it I spoke, and the service was lovely her 4 girls did her so proud!

There were loads of little signs, so I decided to contact a medium and I found a friend of a friend Teressa. She provided great evidence from my gran but also said I had the gift to do what she does after around 10 sessions I knew I needed to investigate this path more, it was like a calling I couldn't stop thinking about it, so I messaged Jan a friend of my Grans, who knew a lot about "spooks" as mam would call them, Jan said of a circle starting soon "what's a circle?" I asked she said its where like-minded people go to learn how to do mediumship, so I contacted the leader of the circle.

Chapter 5

The Circle.

This is where I thought my journey started! Remember Lisa the crystal lady? Well guess who the leader of the circle was!!! Unbelievable or what.

Lisa is a beautiful, gifted soul and Teacher of so many magical topics, she was the first beautiful soul to use the word PATIENCE on my journey.

We laugh about it now well, kind of it's still a swear word in my dictionary!

In my defence patience is not a strength I possess! But it is absolutely one you need on this journey, as much as I hate to admit it!

The first class me and my mum (yes, I made her come with me) met the group we were all new, yet they had spiritual experience and all I had were a few signs, songs, and the desperate need to talk to my gran! You could say I had the passion! If I had known then what I know now maybe I could have

*benefited more from the class, because we are all
different and I agree I am a challenge,*

*But I believe I learnt the way I was meant to
because if I hadn't then I wouldn't have met the
wonderful people that are in my life now!*

*Lisa said we were starting with a meditation; I
have never done a meditation and all I could think
when my eyes were closed was who's watching
me and why am I not seeing anything!*

*After the meditation Lisa went around the room
one by one asking what we experienced, people
were saying they saw faces, angels, heard words
and when she got to me all I could say was I saw
purple! I was quite excited that I saw a colour, but
this was before the others had seen actual angels!*

*I was instantly gutted and felt like spirit did not
want me there, because I did not see anything!
Lisa assured me that purple was a beautiful
spiritual colour and now purple is what I see all my
visions in, the next week my mother couldn't make
it, but I still went. In the meditation this week I
saw a triangle with an eye in it an actual eye and it*

opened I was so excited I don't think I followed the rest of the meditation! My heart was

beating so fast, I wanted to shout out there and then I see an eye an actual eyeball! But I managed to wait until the meditation had finished. Nobody could explain the eyeball which was frustrating I wanted to know what everything meant! Even to this day I see things I don't understand and that's ok, spirit can show up and be mysterious, this is my response now ha-ha!

I would try to communicate but my mind is so powerful, it was as if there was an off switch, to the receiving part!

As the weeks went on, I would live each day counting down the days to Wednesday, I'd meditate like my life depended on it, and would see colours and sometimes faces but nothing made sense to me why am I seeing these faces if they don't speak or tell me what they want? I'd message Lisa who would say, "ask them who they are," to my response, "I do! But I get nothing and then they're gone" (here it comes!)

"Have patience Rhian, it will come in good time."

Oh, my word it was like nails down a chalk board, how could one word cause me so much discomfort! I mean now I understand which is why I'm writing this book for you, I want you to know if you have the passion, the want, the need, and determination then you will do it and succeed,

I remember buying book after book and reading them thinking this is going to help and all it did was frustrate, or confuse me even more.

"Ask your guide to join you!" they would say,

"Now ask them to talk" by this point I was thinking is there a plug in my crown chakra, because nothing worked! I joke now and say I nagged spirit so much to let me in that they had a group meeting and the divine source said, "just shut her up and let her in will you,"

"If you want something bad enough then never give up! The best things happen when you least expect it."

In group we would have a lovely time and were introduced to a few different techniques, but every week I left feeling deflated because I just was not getting anywhere, and I wanted to know it all there and then, I'm also awful to compare myself even now! This one time we did a meditation and I remember seeing the purple and then all of a sudden, my eyes started to flicker like mad my heart would beat so fast, and coming towards me was this man with wings, yes it was an angel, I could feel the excitement rising up through my body, but then he started to bow down to me and as he did this there was this green energy glowing all around him, then he left, I thought I was going to combust right there on Lisa's couch! The angel I now know was Archangel Raphael the healing Angel, all Archangels have a purpose,

It went quiet for me again then, that's how my development worked I would have nothing for weeks then a beautiful visit or connection!

I came home one day and on the floor of the bathroom there was this!

I know it's not the most hygienic of signs, but wow it is undeniably an angel.

After a few more weeks of feeling so low in my self-esteem and a few more words of "patience" where one time I thought my eyes were going to get stuck at the back of my head because I had rolled them so far, I came to the decision to leave the group. I was sad and often wondered if I made the right decision,

A few weeks had passed,

I was invited to join another circle, I debated but thought was the universe guiding me.

What it was doing was keeping Leighann in my life we met in Lisa's, and it was like we always knew each other, the new group placed Susan in my life, someone who was pretty much exactly like me, looking for her calling in this life and she too didn't get on well with "patience".

I enjoyed my time there too but again I wasn't getting anywhere every week I felt deflated leaving group, I'd get so upset because I really wanted to help people like I was helped, after my gran died.

The word patience was used a lot here too!

little snippets of things happening but nothing like the rest or at least I just didn't understand it! I was getting images on my glasses, I was seeing faces on the floors, walls and even on people's skin! Nobody understood it, they said spirit can show themselves in any way, I will share some of these images throughout the book! The group was progressing they were so open to receive, and they knew exactly how it worked, I just couldn't receive anything, I was waiting for that moment where I would hear a voice, one day they had a visitor to the group who was a medium, he came over to me and said "you are super spiritual aren't you" I was speechless, "I wish" was my reply he said he wanted to work with me, but that didn't happen!

This made me more frustrated that strangers could see this in me, but I couldn't!

I now know yes, I am a spiritual person, being spiritual does not mean being a medium or being psychic, it means you believe in things that you cannot see, feel or touch (well you can to a certain extent) it is not all about connecting with lost loved ones it's knowing your place in the world, and in the universe.

After a few months I left that circle too, I had come to the conclusion, that I was meant to develop on my own and that is what I've done!

Back to May the 4th 2018 this was when I had my first spiritual vision!

I was sitting in my room one night and went to take a selfie with Freya when the camera was facing the wrong way, the flash was on, and I saw orbs actual orbs flying in the doorway! I was ecstatic! This led to so many other images especially on my ceiling and in my glasses! I saw an old man, old lady, a young girl with fairy wings who later on was given to me in a reading they described her exactly as I saw her they said she was a daughter I lost, at the time I didn't know I'd lost a child but I understand it now, I saw images like this for years and people thought it was strange how I'd see them in the reflection of my glasses I even saw mam! I will add these images throughout the book. I hope you can see them.

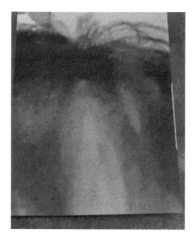

A beautiful Angel on my forehead.

People in the group's would tell me they thought I was going to do amazing work one day, and work with angels, as much as I loved hearing this I think it put that expectance in my mind, I wanted it there and then and things were moving way to slow for me, I wasn't understanding then how I was receiving messages or visions, I actually thought when people said they saw an angel that they saw a actual angel In form in front of them like seeing me or you, when I questioned some years later they say it's like an outline or a blur and they just know, or they see it in their mind like if I said to you now picture a green shiny apple you can see it yes? This is another way that spirit show you it's your mind's eye, well I'm still trying to understand this skill myself, but I do know now that I am a Clair-cognizance, I will see a triangle for example and tent will pop in my head, this is spirit giving you symbols. It's like when you have a memory like a walk on the river for example, but they are not your memories they are the person you are reading for so ask them if they understand it, trust me it's taken me a long time to figure this out! Now I'm aware of it though I work hard to develop it,

CHAPTER 6

Reiki

Reiki in a nutshell is a spiritual healing channelled from spirit through your physical body and through your hands,

This is a therapy that I personally believe should be taught and received in person, you learn all about Dr Usui, Dr Hayashi and Madame Takata, the three Reiki masters, Dr Usui being the main discoverer of Reiki,

Being told once, I was a healer, my overactive inpatient-ness led me to do a reiki course! Lisa is the Reiki master teacher so off I went to her home again. It was so lovely to see her and if my overactive inpatient ness wasn't a part of me, I would not have done the course, and I would not be where I am now, so my advice is to embrace your impatient ness people!

I completed Reiki 1 and loved it but decided after a while it was not for me! Ha that is what I thought!

Anxiety remade a big appearance, and we went back to hypnotherapy and Andrea said, "itis very deep Rhian it hasn't done anything this time," you see if you don't believe something is going to work, then it doesn't! remember that!

I got home and Lisa messaged me "what's wrong" she said I told her, and she kindly offered Neve a reiki session, but Neve refused to leave the house, Lisa suggested I do it so I got the bed out and asked neve to get on it, Freya my youngest went over grabbed her hand and made her get on the bed, I didn't do what I normally do I went straight to the head I imagined pulling out all this negative energy and replaced it with colourful phrases like purple for strength, yellow for happiness and green for healing. I was asking her guides and my angels to please help lift her. I finished and was emotionally drained, Neve sat up and I said are you ok? She said it was strange and she told me she saw purple; yellow and green colours and she saw a phoenix!!!!! I was amazed and at the same time felt like a superhuman, for the first time ever!! I knew then I had to do my level 2 in reiki is this my calling my purpose. I could actually help other people! The next day I was having my hair done and I couldn't get an answer when I

phoned Neve, and all things were going through my mind, I sped home and she wasn't upstairs next thing she comes out of the shower fully clothed in school uniform I calmly asked if she was ok, and she said I'm going to school! I remained calm and said OK let's go so I took her, and it was the proudest most relieving experience so far, did reiki do this? It was the angels and the powers of healing; from that moment I knew I was getting help from them. Lisa booked me in for level 2 and I completed it and opened,

"A peaceful mind" name chosen by Neve!

It was quite successful I renovated our garage into a beautiful reiki room and a few of my craft customers came for a treatment and loved it!

When people have a treatment, they also would have a spiritual experience they see, hear and feel spirit yet once again in came the frustrations, I wasn't experiencing these things, I felt it was my job to know everything (but no it's not,) I couldn't help thinking something was wrong with me, I'm doing all this work, and I'm still no further advanced, sounds silly to some but for me it's my destiny to be on this path and fulfil what I started out to achieve. I loved Reiki and the results that people would have that feeling of pure calmness and relaxation, some would say they could feel the tense energy literally pour from their body, it was a true gift and honour to be a part of that with them, but I couldn't help feel this just wasn't enough for me I always wanted to know what's next, am I just a channel to bring these experiences through for people without me understanding it myself?

Patience *people would say it'll happen when its time, but I felt it was time there and then and although I knew I had lots of growing left I just wanted to start growing already!*

I gave a lot of free sessions, if someone needed it I would do it and one day I gave a free absent healing session to an acquaintance, absent healing is no different for me I do exactly the same as if you were in the room actually I feel the energies stronger maybe it's because it's just me and no pressure, well I was doing this healing and it was angelic reiki when all of a sudden I started talking these words and as I was doing this I started crying uncontrollably I was channelling directly from spirit,

"Love is the strongest energy of all, and when we lose love, we lose a part of ourselves. But love does not have to come from a partner, it can come from the universe, family, and friends. But the most powerful love of all comes from within for if you don't love yourself then you don't allow others to love you either."

Beautiful, isn't it? I printed it out and it hangs proudly in my treatment room!

Another session was with a regular client of mine and I was seeing mermaids in the ocean, the lady herself is spiritual and felt a real strong presence in the room. We talked a while and I too could feel this energy, I was then being guided to use my pendulum, as I picked it up there was a definite energy holding the pendulum with me, we started to ask questions my heart was beating so fast as the pendulum started to move, it was so strong!!! I loved it, the person coming through was a friend who passed tragically even though the pendulum can only answer yes and no it worked perfectly fine! An auntie also came through with validations.

At the end of the questions, we were reminded of the mermaids and my client still could not understand and then I started to get a memory of how mam's trinket popped into my head when I was having a reading once, almost like she placed it there, (which I now know she did) well with that she goes oh my god! My auntie collected mermaids Rhian, they were everywhere, and then there was a huge bang in my room, and I got the thought message delivered! Mrs Clair-cognizance was there all along!

This was such a wonderful experience we were both absolutely delighted,

This just left me hungry for more though and I knew it was my calling to help channel through messages, this is it I thought it is a breakthrough….

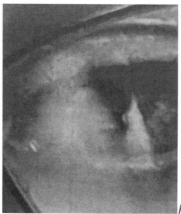

here I see a man from the napoleon era talking to a dog, maybe this was a clue to my future? Taken 2019.

Back to Reiki!

How wrong was I! this was a one off and not long after came covid! And the world stopped, but for me I was relieved. I closed temporarily.

But still offered absent healing to clients,

Then one day I tried one of my own meditations that I had written for my online hypnotherapy course, I somehow talked myself through a meditation it was like it was not me talking, it was my higher consciousness talking me through this calming spiritual meditation.

*So, every week through lockdown I would go live on my page with meditations that I would write, again little did I realise spirit were channelling these through me! I would have 300 views which actually made me feel sick! And I would be so nervous that I would talk a load of nonsense until the channelling started!! But then people would message me saying how much it is helping them this was incredible to hear, I kept at it until the lockdown ended, I now have a small group where I go on and just channel whatever comes in without it being written first yes, I trust spirit and they have not let me down yet! I decided to change the name of my Facebook page to **Spiritual bliss**, I lost my passion for Reiki, for around 6 months and I never thought I would ever feel like I would go back to it, I could do with the money but reiki isn't about money, if your heart isn't in it and the* *intentions to help, heal, listen and care then you cannot do Reiki because it's a beautiful energy that you need to be a clear channel for and I wasn't, so I remained closed. But today I was sitting in the sun, I had finished writing this book and all of a sudden It came over me like a wave, you're done, you're ready, and I knew it, all the work with Nadine, the healing with the animals and this book is why I stopped Reiki, so I could progress in these areas, and I have, I knew I was going down different paths of learning and development, but today I'm ready to start the hands-on healing again, I'm excited to see what happens! I am now back open! and I now understand and trust in myself and my team!*

What I now know! While doing these treatments I would picture in my mind a door opening in my room. I would know the masters stood behind me I thought it was all in my imagination, but I know now it was my inner knowing the impressions that were being placed in my mind,

Chapter 7

Meeting my guides at last!

Throughout all of this I had no idea who my guide was, people would say call on your guide, and instantly my expectations were heightened "is this it, am I going to find out who my guide is" and nothing I was deflated like a pin in a balloon!

When I was in Lisa's group, I kept seeing this man in meditation, he had white hair and would always be around where Lisa was, I couldn't describe him very well as that part of my development and understanding wasn't there yet, he felt like a priest of some kind. Years later I was given the amazing opportunity to do angelic reiki again with Lisa (I said she was my teacher nearly all my training was with her I was definitely teaching her patience!)

Whilst I was sitting on the couch, she asked us to close our eyes and instantly this man reappeared, I hadn't seen him since I had left the group, this time he was behind a table, I told Lisa and she confirmed he was her guide! Result! Now I just have to find my own!

This came in lockdown 2020! A lot of my journey came together in lockdown, peace, quiet, no rushing around the world had stopped and in that stillness my world began!

I started to sit, not meditate just sit in the silence, with no expectations, closed my eyes and just let whatever wanted to come through, come.

I would always protect my room myself and do my routine first. Then I'd put on some calming music and go into the dark, silent, peacefulness of the world that is spirit.

This next part happened over a few sittings.

At first it is dark, then the colours will flow, but now I was starting to feel coolness around me, a feather like feeling may touch my face, then I would see shapes or little blobs of colour that would take the form of people or animals, then I saw a Indian man and I felt pressure around my head as if he was putting a headdress on me, after a while I asked what shall I call you, I kept seeing a white eagle it was all white, I didn't understand it at all, I was researching what the message of a white eagle was and yes it made sense, it came to my attention that the guide was telling me his name was white eagle! And the bird is also him.

I googled him I don't know why but I was amazed when his face appeared on the screen in front of me.

Chief White Eagle.

Throughout lockdown I made it my goal to work closely with him and learn and trust him. Every morning I would light incense, a candle and set my intentions for him to speak through me as I write it down, he never failed, he was always there, here are some of the wise words that he shared with me.

"It is not how quick you get to your chosen destination; it is what you learn in the way."

" Timing is the essence of all that is good."

"You have all you need, you are a small boat in the centre of a huge ocean, some boats will follow others, some will just drift through the ocean, some boats will sink, but your boat will lead, set the boundaries, lead by example, share the light, share the truth, do this with love, validation, empathy and kindness be that light in the storm lead the last boats to the lighthouse."

"We can't change the world in one day, but we can change our world one day at a time, don't let the negativity of other's embark on your own journey, be true to you, one day at a time."

"Life is a like cup of lemon and honey, the lemon is bitter the honey is sweet, but together they make a perfectly balanced cup of tea you have to endure the bitter, to appreciate the sweet."

"It's important to have expectations for yourself, but it's the intentions that count, intentions must oversee expectations."

These words of wisdom really did help me at crucial points in my personal journey.

White Eagle is my main guide, I have many others which make up my spiritual team, do I see them every time I connect? absolutely not, do I feel them every time no, do I trust they are there? YES! And that is all we need. Trust, in them trust in the uplifting, messages of love that come into your mind that is spirit!

Synchronicity: Do you ever see the same thing over and over? Like 10.10 or 11.11, or maybe you're out on a walk and you pass 3 butterflies in a row, or a squirrel walks up so close to you that you feel theres a reason for it? Well, there is, angels and spirit will do anything to get a message through to you, and as they can't pick up the phone and call you (mainly because they would be inundated with questions from us humans) so they send signs, symbols, and whispers. I talk more about this later on but her is a story about synchronicity,

I was talking to a friend about an experience with a spirit animal guide of mine (yes animals are guides too, I have a few) this one though was an owl! Telling her about an experience I had that I sadly can't share here as it is a video! I was meditating and in my vision I was shown my door it opened and sitting on the steps was this huge I mean 4-foot brown owl! It brought me straight of the mediation but I knew I had to open the door and invite him in, I can see him now the wisdom is oozing from him, anyway I was encouraged to film and so I did, I saw what looked like energy on the ground like white waves, but thought it was my heater or camera so, I started to film around the room and in it came; as if someone had thrown in this array of colour straight at me but that's not all then I see white energy flying around, it was the owl, well as I was talking about this yesterday, I picked my cup of morning coffee up to take a sip, and there was my owl cup! I thought oh ok someone is going to make an appearance, then Freya comes downstairs and starts nagging to take her owl to school, I replied, you don't have an owl, yes I do this went on for a while and what she actually wanted was to take her furby! Then on the radio it was mentioned that a celebrity had adopted an owl, so by now I was really awake and waiting for the message, but this is it, the owl wanted to bring up synchronicity and how important these signs and messages from the animals are. You can look up animal messages on google or by the book that I have

'Animal spirit guides by Steven d Farmer PhD' *It is amazingly accurate.*

Chapter 8

Signs and messages

And I'd give up forever to touch you,

'Cause I know that you feel me somehow,

You're the closest to heaven that I'll ever be,

And I don't want to go home right now.

Signs come in so many shapes forms and objects,
this I found hard to grasp at first that my loved
one would be the robin in the tree, or that feather
on the ground would be sent from a loved one or
an angel I mean robins are everywhere and
feathers fall off bids regularly, spirit know my mind
just like they know yours so they will give you
evidence that you cannot ignore!

For me I was expecting to see my gran in human
form or see a spirit like in films, some people do
but not me I see

and hear differently and oh my it has taken forever to understand it, but here are some common signs that you may have experienced...

Number plates, Music, phrases, cloud images, bumping into someone with the same name as your departed loved one, and my favourite feeling them.

When my grans house sold, I grieved just as much as I did when she transitioned, this house was my home we all grew up here and everything about it was memories, the day I had to go and say goodbye to the little 1 bedroom, cottage broke my heart,

I remember taking pictures of every room knowing that I will never see it again, I felt as if because I couldn't see the house, I wouldn't feel my gran I was wrong again! I sat upstairs crying so much thinking how I can possibly leave, this house is my gran, it is our family, and then my auntie turned up, we had a brief conversation as we were both upset, I left for home. I got to the car and the radio came on, and there was a song I could practically hear mam singing the words to me here they are,

Iris by the Goo goo dolls, the words couldn't have resonated with me any more than they did in that moment.

"And I give up forever to touch you, 'cause I know that you feel me somehow, you're the closest to heaven that I'll ever be, and I don't want to go home right now."

"And all I can taste is this moment and all I can breathe is your life, and sooner or later it's over I just don't wanna miss you tonight,"

"And I don't want the world to see me 'cause I don't think that they'll understand, when everything's made to be broken I just want you to know who I am."

I was so lost, I was so confused, I was grieving, lonely and nobody understood me, I didn't even understand me! I missed my gran so much yet I knew she was around but that didn't help, I just wanted to talk to her, to see her and hug her.

Those words hit my soul, I was in the very beginning of my awakening and very lost and confused to who I was, what my purpose was and what would my abilities be, I knew she was with me in the car in the house and I cried so hard, I was driving home now and the song was ending then the number plate in front of me read E.B.P Elizabeth Prince known as Betty, Elizabeth Betty Prince is what was whispered in my head, such a special gift it is to be awakened to the signs spirit send us no matter how delicate.

I ask spirit about the common signs like robins, butterflies, dragonflies etc. and this is what they have said.

"We are energy, which means we can take any form! We can shape clouds, we can appear on any surface, we can

step into any living host for a few moments when your energy anything is possible, we can fly with the dragonfly or become the dragonfly long enough for you to notice, we also let you know it's us by giving you that thought, we are anywhere you are. when we pop into your mind or memory this is us, we are impressing these memories on you,"

The images below are of cloud spirits and Paddie on Poppie's back.

So, when you are in a calm trans like state, for example doing the dishes! When your mind drifts off, and you are in automatic mode, and you may feel or start remembering a person or animal that's them taking advantage of the opportunity to pop in and say hello!

Chapter 9

Abilities.

We all have the ability to connect with spirit, the difference is how we connect and what our strongest ability is, my strongest ability at first was self-doubt! Don't do this! do not doubt yourself because it just prolongs your journey! But saying this, my journey has definitely made me more aware of the person I am, and it has helped me re-live and release some skeletons I didn't actually realise were living in the closet! My mind is extremely powerful, not just with determination but with putting myself down this is another reason why I'm being encouraged by my team to write this book, reliving my own journey, I really am seeing how amazing it has been so far and yes, I'm only a few years in!

Clairvoyance was my first ability! As I've said numerous times now, this is how spirit first presented themselves to me by seeing spirit in my glasses, I have a few images that I can share with you that are undeniable! You see I was so hard to convince that this was real that I can promise you everything I share is 100% my truth, I could never lie or give false information because I personally know how these messages can affect someone.

I have hundreds of images of spirit, some are so clear where others disappear after I have seen it, it's as if they pop in and then just disappear one that always sticks in my mind is an image of a child in my glasses, I don't know the child, but I believe she would have been mine, remember from earlier in the book, I would have named her Ava, she was so clear and looked no more than 18 months old, she has been quite present in the start of my journey. One night I was in bed and just drifting off, and when I sensed spirit, it would freak me out, because it was always at night, and I would be a little scared! I think if your heart doesn't beat out of your chest at first then somethings wrong! At the bottom of my bed stood my gran and Ava, I didn't see them with my physical eyes but the impression in my mind's eye (this was a whole new ball game that I didn't understand) Ava was saying now, can we now?

And my gran said no its not time! And they were gone!

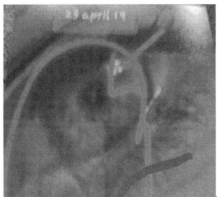

A child.

The next day my guinea pig Winston died, and I swear they were there to take him, but what was I not ready for? Hearing, seeing or something else I still don't know.   I have so many stories and experiences to share which is why I've started the book so early on in my journey, determination pays off eventually, never give up on your dream!

Guides would regularly make themselves known in my hair or glasses my arms, floors walls yes it sounds crazy but it's all true! Orbs oh wow orbs were a huge thing for me I would be the orb hunter, any chance I got off the lights would go on went the camera and wow amazing I'd screenshot them and catch faces in them, rarely recognized them and would never get any information

from them but always thanked them for visiting, try it put your video camera on and the flash and start filming some may be dust but flashing coloured orbs are my favourite.

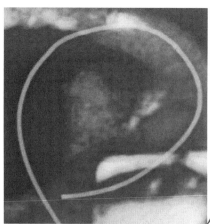

A MANS FACE

No matter how you see spirit do not dismiss it, they are just preparing you, the last thing your guides want is to scare you, because the work they have for you is important, so a relationship of total trust is needed, if you work on a lower vibration, please be careful of the energies you bring in,

Spirit is so eager to talk to you especially loved ones, which brings me to my next story, be ready for a giggle!

My lovely friend Hayley, who I mentioned earlier in the book, has a cat named Klaus, he's a funny old thing well I thought I'd put him in a group for a reading let's see what animal communicators can pick up off him,

He had quite a few messages one which was so detailed I will only put a few specifics here,

"Church, Christmas carols, a pipe and a tipple, yellow blooms for you I love you, challenging times are here, new moon arising, simpler times focus on

the love, Bastard!! oops sorry dear but leave it behind you, life is short live for the future,"

Well Hayley thought the following,

"How, can Klaus go to church and smoke a pipe it doesn't make any sense to me at all he is a cat!"

And oh yes, she was serious, so after I sat down to explain that it is not in fact Klaus going to church but your Gran, she still didn't understand,

Spirit will use any opportunity to get a message through to you, so if they see it, they will take it, they knew Klaus was linked to Hayley and they also know that Hayley is

scared of spirit and will never go to see a medium as she's worried of bad news, (mediums should never give bad news! If you work in the light / high vibrational energy only love and upliftment will come through, unless it is needed for progression.) So as spirit know this, they used the opportunity to talk through Klaus with a good friend of mine Audrey, on a pet communication group, knowing that I would walk her through it and yes, the message made total sense! As I previously explained in the beginning of the book,

Her grandparents were simply using that link that Klaus provided to tell Hayley they love her; they are aware of what has gone on and they are supporting her.

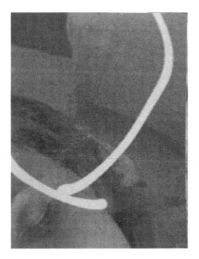

This was quite strange we were on a trip to west midlands safari park I felt the energy in the premier in room and look at this man over Freya's face, I didn't sleep much that night!

Chapter 10

healing

Healing with spirit!

Then came the healing ability, yes this is too the work of spirit they use our body as a channel to bring through the healing that's needed, so never think to yourself I'm just a healer, this is a privilege and an honour that spirit see you as a clear pure channel for them to work through!

Healing will always be my number 1 because it is in everything I do and everything I believe in! even card readings healing is sent through to the recipient, we all have the ability to heal, think back when you were young, and you were ill that gentle touch from your caregiver on your forehead felt more soothing than the medication! When you fall and your mum or dad only would walk by your cut and you'd instantly move because you could feel the energy off them touch you knee, we are all sensitive to healing and energy it's just we choose to ignore it.

My healing journey started with Reiki, which opened the door to the healing world! but now I work with my beautiful friend Nadine, myself and Nadine are being taught by spirit new ways of healing, and it is amazing and my favourite time of the week! We have such a giggle as spirit bring in humour to lighten the intense work that we do, I cannot go into the work we do but it is a privilege!

One time I was talking on the group message chat with another admin Audrey who I mentioned above. We were just chatting about this and that, when I felt this huge energy come over me, it was incredibly strong, and my hands started to heal! I instantly said to Audrey can I message you privately, she agreed so we continued, I told her what was happening, and all these feelings and visions started to come through she knew every person I described, and she understood totally the words of comfort that were being brought through, I said sit comfortably and let in the healing, it was strong she felt it, Audrey lives in Canada, so it shows energy can reach anywhere because spirit is everywhere! This was a new experience to me, but I've had a few since then and each one has been incredibly welcomed.

Healing is such a wide area, we all do it every day when we speak! Or listen, you are helping people heal, when you smile at someone it can lift their spirits, when you start a conversation with a stranger, it may be just what they needed to hear that day!

With me it comes in meditations, talking, listening, reiki and I work with the angels and light beings to heal, angel energy is so pure and so strong it is incredible. When I'm channelling an energy for someone quite often, I will feel the angels come in and I know healing is needed, so I stop what I'm doing and ask them to just relax and trust, and we go into the calm and when that persons ready, they receive the healing, For me the experience is just as rewarding, my hands feel like there's a huge heaviness in them and I feel directed sometimes to a certain area, and other times I just hold the light for the energies to work through me,

Clients are left amazed, calm and usually cry a lot as the healing is about releasing what no longer serves us, it is no joke and it should not be taken lightly, if you go into healing make sure it is because you have a passion for it because so many do reiki now as it is very popular! We have witnessed people in fairs doing reiki, with 1 hand

on the person the other on their phone this is not reiki, reiki deserves respect, dedication and love as does the client on the bed!

Reiki releases blocks of dense energy, it has so many benefits,

Reducing:

- *Anxiety*

- *Stress*

- *Lack of sleep*

- *Tension*

- *Pain*

- *High blood pressure*

- *Nerves/panic*

And so much more like I've previously said people would have a very spiritual experience here I don't know if it was my room, me, or the person but it is a brilliant treatment.

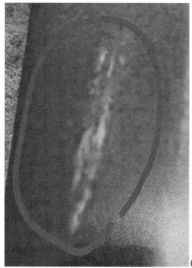

Chief White Eagle my main guide, caught in my hair!

The next ability was Clair-cognizance, which is a knowing, this is by far the most challenging for me because it requires a whole bucket load of trust and self-trust too! And this is how I work now, spirit put all this information in my head and I have to then speak it, my memory is the absolute worse, and as spirit know this as they know us better than we know ourselves they have adapted how I work to suit me and benefit those I work with, so when I started to receive a message this way, I would receive it in sections, spirit would give me something and until I passed it to the receiver they wouldn't give me anymore, it took me a while to understand why they were doing this as nobody else seemed to be working this way, a few members would comment why are you working this way? Most members would meditate and connect then relay what they got, but with me meditation is not an option as I simply fall asleep! So, I close my eyes set the intentions and incomes the energy, they show me something and until I give it, then they do not give anything else, but as soon as I give that I get more! It can vary and I definitely can't connect to every pet! You can see more of the sessions in the back of the book.

Chapter 11

Communication and how it works with me.

Gracie and Frank! My most memorable session to date!

I was browsing through the group I was on, and I saw Gracie but what stood out to me more was the man and French bulldog type dog on the grey blanket behind her, I knew I had to connect, here's what happened.

(Some of this has been cut short as it was over an hour session)

Me: hi, can you understand a man and French bulldog type dog?

Melissa: yes, I had a pug that passed in 2016 so the French type makes total sense and the man I feel is my grandfather who loved Gracie!

Me: ok I don't want to freak you out, but I see them on the grey blanket behind Gracie. He is saying he was there to meet Gracie and the pug was too, I'm being shown Gracie running up the stairs confirming she is fit and well. By any chance did you play hide and seek with Gracie, random I know but she's had me say, Gracie where are you? And I find I'm looking for her, then I see her head pop up,

(Now the me in this scenario was thinking oh wow this is awesome,

But the myself was thinking, is this real am I imagining this,

where the me was saying Rhian, you are actually seeing this it's not a though you are seeing it, give it just give it!)

Back to the session:

*Theres a small white dog coming in now dark ears
darker face,*

*Melissa, everything you are saying is dead on!
When we would come in we would say "where's
Gracie?" and her head would pop up and we could
hear her tail wag hitting the couch.*

My mom had a westie! Who passed 6 years ago,

*Me. Gracie is making me feel really cam now, she's
telling you she's fine don't worry about her, she
will miss you terribly but she's safe and at peace
with your grandad and all of these animals.*

*(Myself ,pipes up again!) Am I really getting this
information how do I know this?*

spirit because we are giving it to you

me just keep going!

*Can you see now how my mind played a great part
in the delay of my development are you confused
yet?*

me. I've a beautiful cat now lying down looking like the Prince or Princess of all cats, I want to say tabby and fluffier than the regular cat,

do you feel pressure on top of your head towards the front I feel it is your grandad look out for that and the word kiddo?

Are there trees around you or where you walked Gracie?

(I was shown long pillars in a row and got the word trees in my mind, so I thought what have I got to lose let's just trust it)

Melissa. the cat could be one of many I have been helping with rescue the past few years, and I have lost a few, we also rescued a cat a month before Gracie passed who we call the queen with a big fluffy tail that could be what you are seeing and yes to the pressure I feel and my grandpop did call me kiddo! seriously this is more than I ever expected cannot thank you enough! As for the trees yes! Gracie was quite the traveller, she's been to Disney with trees we have trees in the backyard here, and we lived in VA last year we had trees all around the interesting detail is Gracie was blind for the last four years the fact you see trees is amazing.

(Me interrupts, Oh my god! How is this happening? Is this really happening I saw poles I got trees and look how important that was, thank you so much for helping me spirit!)

And kiddo, I am so happy!

Me: me too this is new to me as well!

So, what came next blew my mind I was actually in a car, and it was moving. I was seeing images fly past me like I was on the road.

Me: can you understand why they put me in a vehicle I have to say vehicle not car (when I went to write car they made me delete it and write vehicle) could be another form of transport maybe? and I'm going down this long road either side of me are mountains or cliffs or something and I see the moon too, your grandad came right up to my face and then I was in this vehicle

Melissa: Yep, that was my grandpop I took him for a road trip to where he grew up and lived. It was about a four-hour ride into the mountains of PA. That morning I switched cars because my air conditioner stopped working. The car I pulled up in to pick him up was a Volkswagen Beetle. He walked up to the car and said I see we are travelling in a sex machine today. (This made me laugh out loud I could feel his character so humorous) the fact you are reading my animals and my relatives is amazing I see signs of Gracie but felt I needed to post her today and now I know why!

Me: he's waited a long time for this and he's like you'll do kid ha-ha but I don't mind I'm grinning like the Cheshire cat here! was he a joker by any chance?

Melissa: oh yes, he was a joker!

(As I was sitting on the sofa, I was feeling grandad sitting by the side of me on my white stool, I now know he was, and the impression was real!)

Me: I'm sitting here, thanking him for choosing me and saying how honoured I am, and I said if they're all like him I won't mind hearing spirit, it would be a breeze! and literally he blows on my face the left side. I turn round to look and see my face in the mirror in the cupboard and I nearly s**t myself pass the whisky! so yes, he is so much fun please know, his sense of humour is very much alive.

Melissa: I am so happy to hear that and that he is helping you today as you have helped me so much!

(Now this was it, this was when I knew spirit were teaching me or at least proving to me that what I was thinking was happening was in fact happening)

Me: I am asking him to speak his name to me, but my mind is saying Frank, but I know it is my mind, next thing he's in front of me and he's drinking from a mug he's quite amazing! He says tell her the day I left was hard for you all but no I'm here I'm watching every day and please know I've all your food babies I'm so very proud kiddo you always did me proud!

Melissa: his name was Frank!

(I nearly joined Frank I thought my heart had stopped beating)

he was always at the bar because that was his social hour. He was a bartender for a time too, so the mug makes complete sense you my friend nailed it!

Me: oh my god I cannot believe his name is Frank!!!!! I've said goodbye now as I'm feeling drained, and I think Frank would be here all night! I'm so amazed and humbled, he has so much love for you, thank you for sitting with me and taking all of this, you have been amazing.

Melissa: by the way, the dog white with a dark ear and face was our other dog who died in 2015! Thank you so much Rhian I have no words!

Melissa and Frank:

Love is... dedication between child and grandparent

This was how my mind worked, I was at a battle constantly not just with me but with the negative side that my friends is our ego, trying to make sense of it all, our intuition is an old muscle that needs retraining so let the information flow, let it out if it doesn't make sense now it may do another time, and don't forget it may seem weird to you like the poles and the knowing of trees, but to them it could mean everything just like my next example with Flossie and Holly. The more you trust the more you will progress.

Holly and Puppy

I was connecting to a cat named Holly she had not long passed, and the pet mum Flossie was distraught, Holly was a cat that she had forever 20 years! No other pets Holly was giving beautiful evidence, but I kept getting a dog a puppy's face and I knew Flossie did not have a dog So, I finally asked can you understand why I am getting puppy?

Flossie replied oh my god my husband keeps saying the next cat we have I want to call it puppy because he thinks it would be so cool! But I am in no way ready to have another cat, a few months later the lady rescued some abandoned kittens, and after a long battle with her broken heart, she adopted one of the kittens and guess what they named it, puppy!

So, my lesson was to give everything no matter how irrelevant it may seem to you it could mean the world to the recipient and if not do not take it back just leave it with them, spirit is never wrong

but sometimes the information may not fit at that moment which brings me to my next message with beautiful Lexi! The lessons kept on coming!

LEXI

A beautiful dog who sadly passed, while her mum Carrie was out, had come through a few times bringing in validation after validation Carrie was

always so open and relieved to receive the messages but there was one that did not fit!

A peacock? Lexi was giving me a peacock, Carrie was confused but said I will hold on to it, Carrie was new to all this spiritual stuff and in this one reading we had guides coming in and the suggestion of seeing a healer as the pain was so intense! Lexi was and is a very high vibrational energy, a great teacher for Carrie her journey ended here in order for Carrie to open to spirit although as we all know we would much rather our loved ones and pets to stay with us but its what's in our soul contracts, any way weeks went by, and Carrie kept in touch that she was going to see a healer the closest one was an hour away! What happened next blew her mind and brought her to instant tears but total belief that Lexi was in fact guiding her, as she arrived nervous and unexpectant of what was going to happen she went into the healer's home and there in front of her was a beautiful stained- glass window and the picture was of a magnificent peacock!

This story is one of my favourites a true beautiful validation from spirit, and a huge lesson to give everything that spirit give you!

There are so many ways in which you can work with spirit you just have to trust and find the right ways for you.

Chapter 12

Animal communication.

So, as you may have guessed my path took a turn down the animal communication lane, it is the best thing that ever could have happened. Animals have always been a part of my life I have such a huge place in my heart for them. Here is how this path came knocking on my door.

We had our first child Neve in 2004, and Libbie our second child in 2007 but just before Libbie came along we thought let's get a puppy because our life isn't chaotic enough! Along came Paddie a 3-month-old westie from Carmarthenshire, Neve complained all the way home as he was smelly, he came from a farm! I didn't care he was the most beautifulest little thing ever! His first night here we watched lady and the tramp Neve loved Disney still does! that night all we could here was Paddie howling just like lady did, we woke the next morning to find a lot of damage ripped floors, skirting boards and scratched doors! Paddie lived until he was almost 13, he was such a good boy, loyal, trustworthy, and handsome a great teacher to my now 3 daughters Freya was born in 2012 Paddie took his role very seriously of protector and lord of the belly rubs! When Paddie was 12 we took him to Garw -Nant, a beautiful country park in Brecon we spent a few hours there he'd been there many times, but this was different I could tell he knew it would be his last time here, as I was getting Freya into the car Paddie sat on the banking, taking in the scenery,

I paused and observed and there came that knowing, he's taking it all in he knows he won't be visiting here again, that oh so familiar lump is

*back in my throat and the journey home was
quiet. Like we all knew he was saying goodbye to
this place that he loved so very much! 2 months
later Paddie passed away, it was a Monday night
and I watched him in the kitchen he seemed to be
having an episode of some sort, I ran out and
called for my husband, we held him and got him
on the sofa, I instantly called on the angels for
healing and was surrounded by this beautiful
purple light as was Paddie, the energy was so
incredibly strong I had tears running down my face
and every now and then Paddie would lift his head
up to check on me, as I was healing him I felt all
these lumps that had not been there before, and I
knew it was time to make that phone call, I
phoned the vets and asked for an appointment for
Wednesday Andrew was still thinking we would be
coming home with him but I said no this is it I can't
let him suffer he's ready to go, Wednesday
morning came and Paddie wasn't in his usual spot
on the stairs for the first time in I don't know how
many years he didn't sleep on top of the stairs,
when we went to go to the car he wouldn't walk
he knew and I now believe he had already started*

*to transition, when the angels came to heal him
they took part of him with them, on the way to the
vets I see him in the clouds and I say to Andrew
he's there already, the transition with euthanasia
was as peaceful as can be we held him, and I told
him to visit me and that he will always be my best
boy! Our hearts were broken inti a million pieces
I've never felt pain like it, now we had to tell the
children! We left the vets alone and there still in
the clouds is my best boy and this is how he shows*

*himself to me regularly, a few days passed, and
paddies urn turns up as I take a*

*picture there in the
reflection of my glasses is Paddie and my gran
together,*

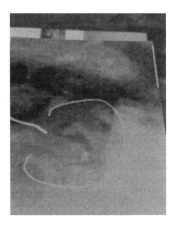

it was so clear to me but not to everyone else but that's because I'm open to spirit, you have to believe if you want to receive! On the Sunday I needed to pop to the local shop, I hadn't been out or spoke to anyone since Wednesday it was august and 27 degrees out so really warm, I went to the shop grabbed what I needed and left without seeing any one I knew, when I got home the house was still, the girls were upstairs and Andrew was up the garage doing work, I was unpacking the bags when this deep male voice from behind me said "is it raining?" I turned round and answered "are you mad? its unbearably hot" then the penny drops there's nobody there, I call the girls and their all upstairs I go up the garage which is 15 meters from my house with 2 closed doors in between us and Andrew was sawing wood he thought I was mad! I come back down and knew it was Paddie every time we would take him out, we would say "is it raining?" because he didn't like the rain!!!!! This is unbelievable how can I communicate back to him? I had to find out how to do this, so I took to the internet, which then led me to the inspirational lady Karen Anderson author of "The amazing afterlife of animals" and "Hear all creatures" these books helped me so much with my grief what happened next was incredible.

I joined her group on Facebook, it was comforting and what I liked was she would personally reply to my comments on how much her book helped me, in June 2020 right in the middle of lockdown Karen invited us all to join her animal communication practice group, I thought great I can finally get a message from my boy, what I didn't realise was I was expected to read animals too! Here comes that pressure again that negative nelly that we all have sitting on our shoulder instantly building a brick wall over my right brain! The right brain is our spiritual brain the left is our thinking our ego you know the brain that talks us out of things, well that left brain controls my right brain and every

day I imagine my right brain growing bigger and taking control, I would give anything to be able to communicate with animals imagine the comfort that would bring to people who are grieving because if you're like me no death is like that of a beloved pets, animals passing hit us in a different place than humans, I don't mean it's worse, although it is for some because like myself my pets are like my children, so losing them is indescribable, and so many people don't understand which is why this part of my journey helping those people is so special to me.

Anyway, I'm scrolling through the page and there's this post, (my first ever pet reading)

27th June 2020. Dusty

"This is my Dusty, I lost him on Valentine's day, it was very sudden and I know he was not ready to leave me," the post goes on and then there was a picture I felt drawn to this beautiful boy but also I felt such sadness in the owner Lindsay's message, I literally thought do you know what I'm just going to sit here close my eyes and ask Dusty if he would like a chat with me, to my surprise and delight I started to see images appear in front of me, I was so happy and at that moment I thought Rhian just give what you see, so I started to type..

"Hi Lindsay, I'm so very sorry for your loss, I'm new at this and still learning but what I see is a huge

tree with loads of leaves, it was magnificent, there was grass and what looked like a sunset, tree stood alone, I see an older dog standing over him and did he used to sit or stand by anyone's shoulders? "

Sounds basic right like so what? a tree and a dog but for me this was a huge breakthrough. I saw these images like a mirage in purple light and like catchphrase my moto is say what you see! This is how my guides have taught me,

Then Dusty decided to give me more!

"I feel anxious, and I see blood, I see him on the floor and there's blood around him, I see someone carrying him into the vets, and I feel a weight in my hands." By now I was emotional and happy all at the same time, the message was more in depth and filled with love from Dusty but here Is Lindsay's response

"Yes, that is a very accurate sign, Dusty became very ill very quick, he started coughing up blood, my husband had to carry him into the vets, I was terrified and hysterical."

Dusty used to sleep by Lindsay's shoulder the tree reference was symbolic to her and a few days after this session the tree image popped up on my phone, so I sent it to her, and in return she showed me a colour by numbers picture of a girl with a dog just like Dusty cwtching up to her neck! Coincidence absolutely not! I made a vow to read 1 animal per day to perfect and grow my skills and I did try to read them, not every animal wants to be read mind! Some were so willing where some were like pulling teeth, I eventually started to see the animal walk into my space and they would bring their human with them, or another pet that had crossed over, I've done around 160 sessions now on pets on this wonderful group, I will add a few of these readings at the end of my book, these animals have all played a huge part in my journey and we had some giggles and lots of tears,

.

Chapter 13

How to Connect to spirit.

So how can you try to connect with a pet or a human? Here's what I do, it's important to remember we all work differently!

- *Say an opening speech. For example,*

*Divine source, universal love light and energy,
I call on you now to step in and work with me, sharing your knowledge wisdom and wonders of the world we live in. I call on my team of guides and angels to protect me and teach me how to connect and receive this beautiful gift, I ask now for the brilliant white light to fill my room and surround me like a protective shield so I can work freely and confidently and to the best of my abilities, I ask for the highest healing and best intentions for all concerned, thank you,*

- *light a candle,*
- *Closing your eyes take three deep breaths,*
- *Go into the silence with the intentions of clearing your mind,*
- *Now think of that person or animal,*
- *Ask them to place their energy on you,*

And that is all I would start with, you may feel anxious or tingly, hot, cold there are so many different things that could happen you may see their energy, try this for a while until your used to the steps write it all down so you can reflect on it, to close the session simply imagine their energy going into a ball of white light and send them back into the universe with love and thanks.,

If your brand new and don't know how to connect in try this small activity,

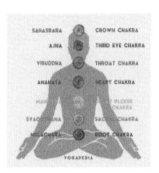

*Sitting somewhere quiet where you will not be
disturbed closing your eyes taken in three deep
breaths calming the mind and now imagining two
gold codes growing down from your feet and into
the earth below attaching themselves to a large
crystal in the centre of the earth, now imagine the
energy from the crystal raising up the chords and
after your body balancing and activating your
chakras starting with your root chakra imagining a
red spinning disc at the base of your Spine above
the pelvic bone, next moving up to the sacral
chakra which is orange in colour below the naval,
now moving on above the navel is a yellow
spinning disc called the solar plexus chakra, and*

above the solar plexus chakra we have the heart chakra in the centre of your chest spinning green, and then moving up to the throat chakra spinning blue, then in the centre of your eyebrows we have your third eye chakra spinning a purple colour imagine now this eye opening, and going straight up to the top of your head which is your Crown chakra this is spinning a beautiful indigo colour or for some people this could be white imagine now a Lotus flower opening out of the Crown chakra and the earths energy is going up like a beam of light connecting you to source, now this white light is creating a big circle around you forming a bubble of pure protection.

You are connected, to disconnect, reverse the exercise bring the light back down and throwing it up into the universe, then ask Archangel Michael to protect you and your home,

There are YouTube meditations on this. Now back to the animals, I was in total awe of this new world that I had found all thanks to my best boy, I did a few readings and I had started to write them down in a book, then I was getting private messages, asking for help to connect with their pet that had passed I was absolutely honoured that people were asking me, and the evidence was absolutely amazing is this really happening to me, I'd go to bed at night and as I would close my eyes I would have these amazing visions of the animals I had read coming close to me it was incredible, July came and I was at the peak of my journey finally a something I can do it's been 3 years of searching wondering if this was all a wish and that I wasn't meant to work for spirit, 3 years of feeling like I didn't fit anywhere and that I wasn't good enough I tried and failed and the following.

- *Crystal ball workshops*
- *Tarot workshops*
- *Sand readings*
- *Automatic writing*
- *Picture reading (these I can do now)*
- *Colour reading*
- *Card readings (but I do these now I know how I receive!)*

- *Mirror readings*

- *Mediumship*

All the above I failed miserably at, and I really did not know where I fitted into this world, I turned to the quietness.

So, by losing my Paddie, and finding Karen I found my purpose, you see I know patience is a hard word to swallow, but what it means to me now is growth! Learn, tick boxes of what you like and don't like, what you can and can't do spirit has put me in all the areas of spiritual work to see where I would blossom, when all along they knew what I was going to do, with my passion for animals and helping people, they have now given me the experience and tools to help others who feel lost and confused, so my advice is take the opportunities that are presented to you, and as I'm typing my guide is joining me with this information.

*" **Opportunities, are presented to you for growth and experience, these opportunities are not all tools that you will learn, but we are bringing in***

new people into your life who will benefit you, help you grow, some will bring knowledge and tips, look at the people who have entered your life since you've been on your journey, would you have met them otherwise?"

So can you see how it works I can tell you now, most of my friends now I would never have met had I not attended workshops, courses, or classes. Even the hypnotherapy course all that time I dedicated, and I never used it but what it brought me was the realisation that I can write and channel meditation which has helped so many people, So, where I thought I had failed and was feeling so useless, I now realise it was all to bring these important people into my life, who have introduced me to others that I now work alongside of! Remember Andrea, well she introduced me to Dee, when I took them up on an opportunity to learn kinetic shift and hypnosis, energy work, Dee then did an angel workshop that I went to and she got in touch with me a few months later to invite me to Jane's angel workshop, oh my god this was the most incredible experience ever,

my first ever visit I sat by a lovely lady called Nadine, little did I know I'd be spending every Monday night with her healing and working, developing but most of all laughing! Nadine is the reason I understand who I am now she is incredible, and she is the kindest person I know! One day Freya decided to put a diamond jewel up her nose! Like you do when your 9, apparently it fell of the wall and landed up her nose, well we tried everything and was dreading a hospital visit, I mentioned it to Nadine while we were working and she said let's look, so psychic surgery it was Nadine could see it she described it perfectly she said ok I'm removing it but Rhian you have to believe I do believe I said, later that night I went down the house as we work over video call, Freya done a huge sneeze and seconds later it came

out the size of a 5p piece!!!!!!

Jane is one of the most incredibly selfless gifted people I know, my first encounter in her workshop was for my Neve, I for some reason mentioned her

*anxiety, and Jane said well, let's heal her, this was
a few years ago now and I wasn't expecting this at
all... everyone joined hands around 15 of us and all
of a sudden I see neve float into my vision I had to
speak I said " oh my god I can see her she's in front
of me" to which an amused Jane replied "well of
course you can I've called her energy in, Neve was
oblivious to it but remained in school for the rest
of her time there, I owe so much to these
remarkable people,*

"Smile and the world smiles with you"

"Be the change you want to see in the world"

" I may have left, but I have not gone"

*I would feel so low on times, like I knew I was
meant to help people and make a change, I knew I
was meant to work with spirit.*

. Words by me

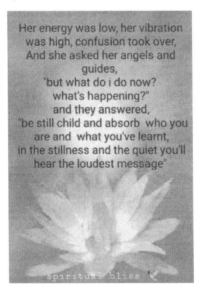

Her energy was low, her vibration
was high, confusion took over,
And she asked her angels and
guides,
"but what do i do now?
what's happening?"
and they answered,
"be still child and absorb who you
are and what you've learnt,
in the stillness and the quiet you'll
hear the loudest message"

spiritual bliss

Chapter 14

An opportunity of a lifetime.

Back to Karen and the biggest opportunity yet

July 2020 a private message from THE Karen Anderson!

"Hey, you, I'm looking for someone to help me run this group as admin, and that person is YOU! Are you interested?"

AM, I INTERESTED!! OH, MY ACTUAL GOD YES YES YES, SIGN ME UP BABY!!!

To which I replied "hi, I would be honoured and privileged to help you with the group," calm right?

Wow how is this happening? to me a normal well normal-ish, girl from Wales, I wanted to shout it from the roof tops, but I did not! actually, this is the first time I have even spoke about the group as I wanted it to be my secret, no pressure, a comfort zone which it is, I feel confident and safe there. I have met so many friends and remarkable people through Karen's group. Karen is such an inspiration and if I am a quarter of the communicator, she is then all the hard work, money, stress, and downer days would have been worth it do you know why, because without all those negative experiences of not being able to do the other things, that other people could, I would never have found something I am truly passionate about and actually quite alright at! Karen is absolutely dedicated to her animals and her role as an animal communicator and pet loss specialist, her book will be at the back of my book it is amazing.

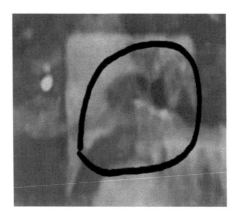

I had no idea who the cute pup and kitty were but how nice it was to see them. Looking at this now I see Poppie!

It is not all plain sailing though! And anyone who says it is, is either a very gifted soul or a little extensive of the truth!

This is me in a nutshell! I would wake feeling optimistic, with all these ideas and by the time I had finished my coffee I had totally talked myself out of it!

Chapter 15

Question time

1. *Can you connect to any animal? Absolutely not! I can connect to those who choose to connect with me,*

2. *Is every message you get mind blowingly amazing? umm no but I wish it were!*

3. *Do you get super clear visions and messages? No, I work hard on my trust, and I do this by trusting my guides with everything,*

4. *Can anyone communicate with animals? Yes! if they put in the hard work and dedication, love, and commitment that they require and deserve and if it is your calling.*

5. *Do your loved ones think you are crazy? Yes, probably but not because of my beliefs, actually a lot of my loved ones know nothing about what I do as I keep it*

to myself, so if they read this book then yes, they probably will think I am mad, but I love and respect what I do so if they can't support that then that's something I will cross when it happens! My family who knows of it fully support me.

6. *What is the highlight of your path so far? Animal communication is my biggest accomplishment and my whole heart!*

7. *Has spirit ever left you? yes and no, spirit seems like they leave you from time to time but they are always there in the background watching guiding protecting, sometimes in the absence of spirit there is growth, so when you feel like it has gone you cannot connect or focus it is because you are being prepared for a new direction or lesson, so in the silence is where we learn the most.*

8. *What is your most memorable experience with Angels? One night I was woken, and I saw an Angel standing in my room, she had long blonde flowing hair like ripples in*

the ocean, there was this golden energy radiating off her and she was just there, I kept telling myself "I am awake, I am awake" it was incredible. I usually work and see

9. *with my eyes closed but this was the first experience and only one to date that I saw with them open!*

10. *Do you teach, your own circle? Gosh no, I'm not ready for that but it is a passion, that one day I will be ready to.*

11. What is manifestation? Manifestation is a *powerful tool, its where you send your thoughts and wishes out into the universe, so if you need an extra bit of cash for your bills keep asking please can you help I will work for it etc and you will find someone will book in or something you have for sale may sell, start small, I manifest all the time, but be careful what you wish for and how you word it! also be careful of your thoughts as it all gets manifested like if you constantly say I never have any luck or*

*I'm never going to win then that is what
you will get!*

*I was manifesting someone to work with me on a
one to one, and money is very tight in my home so
I couldn't afford it, a few weeks ago I was
contacted by a beautiful friend of mine and she
was offering psychic development classes to me
one to one for free, I kid you not I couldn't believe
it, I jumped at the opportunity, what I didn't
realise was this was a huge lesson from my guides,
after a few weeks of classes I was noticing I was
constantly drained, no energy at all, I couldn't
connect to animals or anything, any time I'd try I
would feel like I was going to sleep, I contacted a
friend and instantly she said it's a lesson Rhian you
don't need development your guides have taught
you and you are where you need to be, your guides
are giving you what you asked for but they are
showing you by taking away what they have
taught you.*

*I felt so bad, bad for not trusting my team and
bad because I now had to let down my friend, but I*

thought my guides were rewarding me with this offer, so it was an easy error,

(After writing this I was reminded of an important message whilst in the shower, spirit had tried to tell me in my first session with this lovely lady and I missed it, when we were aligning my chakras, I saw myself, with shopping bags, I questioned it and my friend said their telling you, you have all you need! Was I thinking about this in the shower no, I was thinking about getting the shampoo out of my eyes, so I definitely know that spirit was confirming this for me?)

I let my friend down gently and within 2 days I was back to normal, although the messages were changing, they were becoming more soulful, and after talking with Karen she said I was connecting to the higher selves of the animals.

Chapter 16

Do animals have a purpose?

*Do animals feel, experience and love like we do?
Do they have a higher consciousness?*

*of course, they do animals are sent here to teach
us love, empathy, commitment, and loyalty!*

*Here are some sessions of animals that have
spoken from their higher consciousness.*

***"We can love our pets more than anything in the
world, but to our pets we are their whole world."***

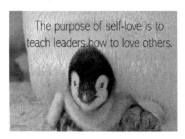

The purpose of self-love is to teach leaders how to love others.

This Photo by

Meet Ruby.

Ruby passed aged 4, and her pet parents never got to say goodbye they didn't know what happened to her, I couldn't resist being a westie mum myself...

I cannot resist a westie especially beautiful Ruby who for some reason I want to call Grace? I see her, she is so beautiful and graceful which could be why I want to call her grace! She comes in with a Garland of flowers around her head, they are like yellow sunflowers. She says mum my time with you was the best I had to slip away and could not bear to see your face so sad, so I went when you were gone! I have an important job to do here! I can't quite make out her role though, she is in nature almost like a leader for the wild animals, ohhh .. (Income the download of knowledge)

she is a guide for many children here on earth that are still carrying the gift she is teaching them she kindness with animals trying to encourage potential abusers to be empathic, this is why she had to leave so soon, her role is so needed and she is saying   because she didn't understand how humans could be cruel she got to visit earth for a short while, 4 years is long for us humans, but for spirit it's like a week, she says (which is crazy?)

She came, she saw, she gathered, she left, but what she experienced was pure love and emotion and that's what she wants every animal to experience so This is why she had to leave so soon because her work is extremely important, she loves you all and thanks you for helping her on her journey also you Lisa made a difference she said you helped her be more determined than ever to bring cruelty to an end.

What an incredible message from spirit! Even as I wrote it, I was thinking is this real is this happening, but this is something I would not ever think of, so I trust 100% that this is a message from Ruby and her higher self.

Lisa's response: hi. Aww Grace. Amazing Grace that is what Ruby is the flower reference is meaningful to me very much, sunflowers my grandson and I planted some seeds last week and only yesterday did I check on them and hey-ho they have sprouted wow she knows this. I also love sunflowers so much that I have them tattooed on me Ruby knew I loved my garden and nature incredible, my sweet girl we did have the best times always protecting the ones she loved, oh my word I always try and help and protect nature and animals I rescued ferrets I had my own ferret sanctuary Rhian. I took in lost ferret and always ended up keeping them she knew I never understood cruelty and she saw me cry so many times over this, she was always there to wipe away the tears I am so touched by this my busy sweet little Angel I'm so glad she's been chosen to spread the love she had so much to give! she gave me so much in four years enough to last my whole life, I'm so glad I helped her and I'm so grateful for this message from her what an amazing little girl I had the pleasure to love thank you Rhian.

Meet Coby another heart breaker! Here is what he had to say to his mum Kat lee!

Such a gorgeous boy, he made a huge impact on your life, he was extremely loyal, and he still is he says listen closely I am the voice you hear; I am the intuition you listen to I am your whole heart and I understand exactly who you are, we have lived many lives together and learned many things. And our journey is in no way over I am all around you. Coby's love for you is incredible, but he makes me

feel like he had a certain role like a bodyguard and teacher he took and still takes his role very seriously, he says but I still know how to have fun. He showed me him tickling you to try and make you laugh you scratch thinking it's a bug or hair on your face but it's him he says he shows me him following you everywhere even guarding you on the loo, he was very quick to come in and talk he has a yellow rose in his mouth a sign of love and upliftment he says in a role between human and dog the human takes care of the dog which you did amazing, but he says the role was reversed for you, he was your caregiver your protector your reason to get up in the mornings he said you lived an amazing bonded life together and know just because he had to go doesn't mean he left!

Kat Lees response: I love your reading with my Cobo, thank you! That is so beautiful I believe everything you wrote is exactly right! exactly right for me right now too! I feel it all in my heart these words, thank you. Wonderful to hear he is the voice I hear, I have been hoping so he is my whole heart and I know we have had many lives together, so many have told me so too! He is so wise and was a beautiful old soul I bet he is following me to the loo he always did that every time just checking on you mum! Was definitely a protector and I am sure that he still is I know this thank you Rhian, Cobo, this is just beautiful!

Next up Colby his message was the first higher-self message I received, and it was so beautiful it had to go in the book.

Colby.

He was your protector here, and he is your protector still, his eyes are amazing such wisdom love and loyalty I'm so very sorry for your loss but

*he says you've not lost me I'm here, we are just in
a different space of time, my time now is bliss
actual heaven and here is where I will wait for you,
but don't rush you have so much more to
accomplish more animals to love and more paths
to travel, time is nothing here it's not me sitting
around waiting and pining for you it's not this at
all I'm simply walking each step with you guiding
you protecting you whilst also being free from the
physical form! that protected yet restricted my
soul, know this I'm free, freer than I ever thought
possible know that I was never trapped I loved my
life with you I miss it but this freedom lets me help
you in ways I couldn't physically, no more tears!
embrace the gift that is life embrace why it is your
here and listen for my advice, my touch, my signs,
love always your boy.*

*I did not realise what was happening when I did
this reading it is extremely powerful! take his
words with love I am in absolute amazement with
him.*

*Candice's reply: I am in tears! Colby was my life all
I do is tell him how much I love him and miss him*

*every day I hold his urn and touches clay paw print
I saw him once waiting at heavens-gate I told him
to go run and play and not to wait for me and that
I would be there with him in time Colby was made
protector but not only to me but to his younger
sister pepper I know in her heart she misses him
terribly he was an amazing older brother he will be
with me always but this heartache I feel will never
heal and my heart will never be whole again he
was my son and I wish I could kiss him and say
goodbye once more I thank you so much..*

*Candice also had a message from her live snake
another first for me!*

Meet Obbie, the albino California king snake!

*Hi Candice, OK I pushed myself out of my comfort
zone here not with a snake but with a live animal!*

*first Obbie said for me to speak because I sat
quietly! I did not know what to ask! so I ask Obbie
what do you like to do? which he replied he loves
to watch you humans go about your day, he labels
my breathing, he's quite comical as I link back in
he says do you think I'm not busy that I just sleep
all day on the contrary I'm a very busy boy,
planning when to eat my food! is he shedding or
due to shed? he's full of knowledge he saying he's
experienced many lives and I'm also getting a
lizard of sorts he wants to experience different
forms on earth he thinks humans are funny busy
creatures, that do things that are not necessary,
he thinks we should prioritise what's most
important living, eating and building a better
world he's happy where he is enjoying a more
quiet life this time not slithering away from
predators (I've never even thought of it like that) I
feel he is going to teach you Candice! thank you
for sharing him with me he showed me fruit do
snakes even eat fruit or just bugs anyway take
care thanks again he is the first snake I have ever
tried to connect with.*

Candice's response: Rhian wow that was a great read I've tried and tried to read him and I can't I feel a block with him communication wise he is actually shedding right now and wants to be left alone I get it though I always put myself in their shoes thinking how uncomfortable that would be! he loves to be out and about in his enclosure slithering around so yes he's a very busy boy we also have lizards maybe you're picking up on one of those he doesn't eat fruit or bugs but the other two do though thanks again!

Looking back now I should have known this was my path, with animals I mean. A few years back I started to get very uncomfortable with eating meat! I mean I used to actually feel like I was going to vomit because to me eating meat was like eating humans I know it sounds mad and I never used to think of it like that, I used to say if we don't eat it then the animal died for no reason, but somewhere on my journey this changed and boy oh boy did I struggle because I love meat, but I physically couldn't do it, it was weighing heavily on my conscience, I cook it for the family though, Christmas I would eat turkey but that's it, until

Christmas 2020 I ate turkey and was convincing myself to just eat chicken then I dreamt about the chickens and woke crying I won't disturb you with what they showed me, let's just say I eat no meat at all, but there are so many alternatives now that it's a lot easier that before,

So, there was one clue how could I work, heal, and talk to these beautiful creatures and then eat them no it is not happening. This does not mean you have to do it though.

Another clue was the healing as I just mentioned, people would ask me to send healing and I would and I'd see the animal come in front of me, when Paddie was ill I gave him angelic healing I saw the angels come around hit was miraculous, and he felt it you could see in his face, Guinea pigs love healing their really responsive to it, I've sat and sent healing to animals and humans while their transitioning and that is a beautiful honour, I've not been with them in the room, but my soul is with them and I talk and send love and healing to see their loved ones turn up to help them cross is extremely reassuring and heart-warming, these are stories I don't tell people but they are part of who I am and it explains my path, this one you may think I'm quite mad I know my children and husband do we do have a giggle though even if it is at my expense, road kill ughh it gets me every time and as we drive passed I hold up my hand and envision the animal going up into the light, this week was a huge hedgehog but what I saw was an angel preparing to receive him with her hands ready, it makes me feel better no living thing should be left on the side of the road, a life is a life regardless what humans think, I believe we can learn so much from animals, and they really are incredible energies whether they're here or in spirit!

For some tips to help you understand how mediumship works I recommend looking for mediums that you can relate to, I am a total fan of, the Long Island medium Teresa and Hollywood medium Tyler, these are 2 incredibly gifted people I have learnt a lot by watching them deliver messages.

My rules for how I work are simple, I always aim to give healing through the messages be positive and uplifting, I always ask for upliftment for the recipient, I don't believe in negative messages and spirit will not relay negativity through you if you're a worker of a higher vibration, I've received many messages that have been on the negative side which I knew wasn't true, what I didn't understand was how someone lucky enough to be gifted would want to deliver such negative messages, but now I know it's because their working at a lower vibration so set those intentions high to start, be the difference and spread your light!

We all work differently this I cannot stress enough I am my own worst enemy comparing myself but this I try to reinforce every time that negative nelly pops in! here is what spirit say:

"If you all receive the same message then what would be the purpose? If you are healing through messages and you can connect a dog a blue ball that blue ball is his favourite toy ever, he was buried with it, then the pet parent would be overjoyed but then the next person comes and

gives exactly the same, can that pet parent heals from the recurring message? No, the next person says I see your dog with a man with a grey beard blue jumper and a pipe, he says I have got him safe! The pet parent is relieved the dog is with her brother, can you see now how we all have these different messages and abilities, because the more we can share the greater the healing and knowledge, and by sharing this information you are making believers out of these people and together the worlds energy will rise".

Long I know but this is how I was taught not to compare myself,

I know this is animal related, but this goes to who or whatever you work with.

Chapter 17

Poppie, Daisey and more about

me.

After Paddie passed I vowed no more dogs, I did not mean it but at the time my heart was broken, but Paddie had other ideas, after all he was preparing me for the new role I was about to play. I kept hearing the name Bonnie. I was saying to him stop Pads I cannot think about this yet, then came the visions and wow not just any normal vision well not for me anyway,

I am in bed and as I am just going into that state of total calm before sleep, my whole vision lights up, the brightest most beautifulest light I have seen, and there I see Paddie walking around my living room healthy happy and watching me as I lie there, heart beating and in total respect for the gift I'm receiving. This happened a few times always at night, then one morning I'm woken and in my head is the word cosmos, repeating over and over again, and there's Paddie, just watching me, at this point I get up to make a coffee, one of my shows are on mike and molly, and its Christmas, the little dog Jim is looking out of the window at the snow and I instantly burst into tears Paddie loved Christmas and how were we going to cope without him, to distract the flow of uncontrollable tears I browsed Facebook, scrolling away and then I see it a dog tree decoration and what was the name? COSMO! I had to screenshot it to prove to the family as they would never believe me!

I found myself looking for a dog named Cosmo that needed a home because that is what I thought the message meant, but it did not it was Paddie and the universe saying it is in my destiny to have dogs.

A few days passed and I was looking at rescue sights and preloved pets, and I saw a add from a local family they said they have a Facebook page so curious I looked, there they were beautiful schichons,

A mix of shih tzu and bichon- frise, there were 2 girls left, that is ok I thought because Paddie was my best boy so a girl would be best, there was orange collar girl and purple collar girl! And oh, my word I had this pull to purple collar girl, I mean I had to have her I cannot even explain it to you now, without even telling anyone else I messaged the owner enquiring and she said someone is on the way to choose noooo I need that pup she has to be mine! I am there with my pendulum asking it if I am meant to have purple dog it says yes and many more questions all yes! The lady took what felt like forever to choose the orange girl, so I instantly grabbed my card and bought purple girl,

then came the panic what have I done is Andrew going to agree is it too soon? 6 weeks and she would be ours; I did not tell them straight away it was a few days; it was a shock but as soon as they saw the picture they were in love.

More visions! This time I would-be lying-in bed trying to sleep, and I knew something was coming in, so I was prepared it's like a wave of energy coming over the body and there I see the pup? And she is sitting on the floor next to her is a beautiful glowing white silhouette of Paddie.

and the pup starts growing, I know now Paddie
sent her to me as a gift and he is going to teach
her and protect her, I had many of these visions
and the day came to fetch Poppie home I cried
again it was 9th of November it was like bringing
home a new baby Paddie only passed on august
21st so it was all so unreal, but she was the best
surprise, and she really did save us from despair,
the visions would still come when she was here id
be in bed I'd close my eyes and id see her looking
at me I didn't understand it at all, but I know she
was linking in with me. We are so incredibly

*bonded, in March 2020 covid arrived and our
caravan holiday was cancelled thank goodness as
Poppie is travel sick! So we decided to get another
pup as company the same owners other dog was
due to have a litter so I got in touch and reserved a
girl, and this is where the most amazing thing
happened, I'm deep in sleep and being chased by
an eagle, I'm on a horse then the eagle hits me on
the back of my head which woke me but eyes still
closed I actually felt the beak on my head!
Incomes the light, I'm still on a horse and I see
bright green grass, I see my children and my
husband I see Poppie there is a gentle breeze
blowing her fur then my awareness is moved and
there are 4 brown legs I instantly know this is
going to be the new pup, the excitement broke the
vision, and I got up, a few days later I have the
message that there are 3 girls and someone wants
2 before I can choose! I said simply I have
whatever girl is left, there were 2 brown and 1
grey, the other lady picked the grey and a brown,
so we were blessed with the other brown and oh
my she was perfect we named her Daisey Belle,
the next day the owner rang me to say the lady*

changed her mind and wanted 2 brown, as they were better to breed no way on this earth she is mine and is our pet not our income! She said it is fine I told her she is yours, 8 weeks passed and Poppie was a little shocked at first, but they are amazing together, I always regretted not getting company for Paddie, so he made sure Poppie was not alone they are my world, Paddie is still my best boy, and he works with me every time I connect

Daisey's 4 brown legs joined the family,

he comes in bringing through the animals, Paddie has brought through many animals in my family to show me they are ok and happy and I've passed the messages on the owners are always relieved and see them in the images I show them too, I don't shout it from the roof tops but for those who I think will accept and be open to it I believe it's my job to put them at ease, I ask only for the animals who parents will understand to come through, because otherwise the animals using their energy and love on a wasted message,

Paddie shows himself in so many ways here are just a few images, The one with Poppie was Paddies birthday I took the picture as they were trying to eat my flapjack!

and wow, I saw a light going through Poppies face and the left side was Paddie even the corner of the yellow cushion took the place of Paddies ear! Spirit always amazes me I do not think I will ever take this for granted, the moment you do it will be gone, spirit deserve respect and love and I believe you should work in the light be a light worker bringing love and light into the dark world that we live in,

Life doesn't come with guarantees of forever,

so don't take things for granted.

Appreciate what you have.

Cherish the ones you love.

Elle Sommes.

There are so many I could write about but then this would be a book on animal communication, which is my love but I really want this book to be more about you understanding that anything you're going through on your path is ok, it's ok to not understand every message that comes your way, it's ok to not know what your purpose is yet, its ok to see things and not understand them, time is all you need.

Chapter 18

Finding your own path.

I believe. Our path starts the moment we decide to come back here, to earth, we are given opportunities to take or to decline, just because something is put in front of you doesn't mean you have to take it!

As we go through life, we learn we grow and we find what suits us and what doesn't, I grew up extremely fond of animals I couldn't bare hearing of cruelty and now I'm even worse my blood actually boils and I never get that pure animal out of my head the difference now is I can connect and heal,

Walking Poppie and Daisey in my local park I clock eyes on this man walking 2 husky dogs, he was holding the lead very tight with no choice for them to sniff the grass etc., he was obviously trying to be the boss! Why anyone would think being evil to animals is cool I don't know but that's just me, any way I watched him as my husband was quickly trying to distract me because he knows I will say something or worse come home with 2 huskies!

Anyway, the one tried to sniff the grass and the owner kicked him and hit him, at this point I was almost sick, I actually felt faint because if that's what he's like in public I dread to see what goes on at home! My husband forced me to walk the opposite way, so I did, preparing myself to come face to face with him as our park is a 1-mile circle! Sadly, I didn't see him he had gone, I worried about this poor dog and didn't know what to do so that evening while in bed I sat and asked my team to step in and help me heal the dog,

What happened was amazing and showed me just how powerful and amazing this journey is if you believe and use it in the right way which is for the higher good!

I started calling in my healing guides and angels and started sending in this healing my whole hands went completely stiff which they do with healing, but it was like a steel pole was in between them I couldn't move that is how strong the healing was and with that the husky was in front of me, a beautiful face that looked like he was smiling, I filled him with love and surrounded him in protection, I did this for a few evenings and I truly believe it helped him, it doesn't matter how crazy something sounds if your intentions are honest and of love then go for it! School wasn't for me I hated it I was the shy kid that people would make fun of I had thick hair and huge glasses, I would cry over anything I was extremely sensitive, but I had fun with my friends always out playing, me and my brother would lie on the roof of the shed watching the clouds and finding all the animal shape clouds and I remember saying look there's a whale that means a whale has just died? Why I thought that then I don't know but now I see so many cloud spirits it's one of my favourite things to see, I worked from the age of 15 in a fruit and veg shop, and loved talking to the older generation so much love and wisdom not like today, the older generation had so much appreciation for life and the little things it offered, I remember my boss Kevin coming out from the office to ask me if that old lady bought anything? No, I replied she came in to see me! He laughed

*and said I'm trying to run a business! But I couldn't
help it they would come in to say hi every Saturday
morning and leave without buying not even a
grape! So, this helped to shape me as a person
along with my mum and gran I believe I'm an old
soul I fitted better with the older generation than I
did with people my age, I've always struggled with
this I just don't have the interests, I feel I'm here to
be a mum to my children and pets a wife to my
husband but also work for spirit to help people and
animals, that's all I'm interested in. I worked in
factories which were horrid but brought me out of
my shell and gave me more confidence, this is also
where I met my husband! I then trained as a
teaching assistant and landed a job in a lovely
school, I worked there for a few years then I had
Freya, I was delighted my final child 3 beautiful
daughters the only problem was I didn't want to
return to work, I wanted to stay home with her
and enjoy every second! Remember when I said be
careful what you wished for? Well after a scary
few months Freya was diagnosed with Epilepsy at
8 months old, and I handed my notice in! we spent
quite a while back and for the hospital to the point*

*the ambulance men knew us! But thank goodness
it was controlled with medication, she is currently
being weaned off it, at aged 9 !Life sends us
challenges that we think at the time are so
horrible, scary and bad and yes they are but when
we are out the other end and reflect back we see
why it happened, if it wasn't for all the events
that had gone on I would not be where I am now I
may not have found this path and have all the
wonderful people In my life that I have, have
people left my life because of this? Probably
they've not told me they have mind, but people
have disappeared on me but that's ok because
others have stepped in, I don't ask people to
believe I don't push it on them, actually now I
rarely talk about it as the things I experience are
so mind blowningly out of this world that people
would definitely think I'm crazy,*

*I love how my life has turned out, I love how spirit
send the people to me that need my help, they
know exactly who to send people who are
struggling to we all have different healing
qualities, I get regular messages off grieving pet
parents and if I can I will link in with them just to*

help the pet mum or dad feel at ease that their baby is safe and happy which they always are, how do I know? Because they show me, they show me who met them and they walk up the stairs to heaven with them, they make me feel what they are feeling which is indescribable pure bliss! Then they show me that they are still with their pet parent look for Himmie, in chapter 22.

Chapter 19

Trust

Trust, this is the biggest lesson you will learn on this journey and trust me you will not be alone if this is something you struggle with because I still struggle with it!

For some it is an easy setup they sit they connect ask for a message and they get it! Sounds amazingly easy doesn't it, I have read so many books which all say ask your guide and they will answer well this just wasn't the case for me! Yes! I trusted my guides and I believed the authors of these books, but this just wasn't how I experienced it! I would try anything to remove what I believed was a block, I'd go for treatments, reiki, healing, you name it I would try it! If someone recommended a crystal, I would buy it I have so many now I could possibly open a stall! I have beautiful angel statues everywhere, but these are my passion they protect my home and keep the house a calm space! But after all this I finally figured it out, yes, these things are tools that can definitely be used for the higher good and for spiritual practices but as for my personal progression and journey the only thing blocking me was ME!

Time is so important! And timing is key, remember the saying the best things come to those who wait, slow and steady win the race, wells it's not about winning but it's about accomplishing your own dreams, when Paddie transitioned I closed my reiki business for a few weeks, one day I had this message on my page,

HI, it's my first time of reiki my friends swear by it, I just need something to calm me down. I wasn't planning on reopening yet as the loss of Paddie was still raw, but something was telling me to see this woman, so I arranged her appointment and yes, the universe was definitely giving me a taster for what was to come!

How spirit work with me and my healing is they encourage people to release their troubles to me they're so shocked and embarrassed sometimes for bursting into tears and it shocks them, but it really doesn't shock me in fact I welcome it

because when we hold in all that tension and upset or worry it will make us ill! Spirit knows you better than you they've been with you through all your lives, and they know when to send you for help, think of them as your own personal counselling team! One of my roles in this world is to listen and help you release what it is that needs releasing!

Back to the client:

She enters a cheerful, lovely lady by the time she got to the couch she was in floods of tears and couldn't understand why as she was determined not to cry, I told her it's the energies I work with they know what you need, so what's going on? The lady had sadly lost her beautiful dog and was having an extremely hard time moving forward, at first, I wondered what the hell spirit was playing at I've just lost my own dog why would they send me

someone who was in such despair how could I
possibly help this person, we talked for ages about
how special the dogs were and how some people
just don't understand, because they are not
animal people, our dogs are like our children and
this lady was grieving deeply, as soon as I said
those words she looked at me and said "is that
what's wrong with me?" "Theres nothing wrong
with you my love, you are grieving for the loss of
your dog it is perfectly normal."

We all grieve differently some relax after a while
where I've had clients 4 years on and they still
grieve for their pets, she was asking me to connect
with her I said I can't, I don't communicate with
spirit I wish I could but it's not happening, we did
the angelic reiki and I asked the dog to step
forward which she did and the lady was so upset,
that I decided to end the session, she came back a
few times and we spoke about her getting another
dog but she was so full of guilt she couldn't and
then she saw I was having a pup, I told her how it
is the only way I could move forward is passing
this love that has nowhere to go onto another pet,

We made progress, and she decided to see a medium, who then told her that her dog was stuck here and hadn't crossed because she was holding her here, I instantly felt angry all this work that we had done over the past few weeks unravelled with one thoughtless comment from someone who took their money and left! I told the lady it was nonsense and that her dog is happily, in spirit and the last thing she would want is to see you in this state, we did the treatment and that was it I never saw her after that, I was so passionate about my beliefs that I lost a client who was making beautiful progress, but then a few months later I see her out walking her new puppy with the biggest smile on her face, and he is absolute

handful, keeping her busy we had a lovely chat and I believe she may have stopped coming now because her girl sent her this handsome chap to keep her busy, this was long before my ac came to light, 9 months to be exact , I feel what I'm doing now is much bigger and more my destiny, so looking back I see by trusting in my guides to accept the appointment when I wasn't ready too really helped this lady because who knows what would have happened,

Spirit will always send people your way just asks them for those who will benefit from being with you,

How I see and hear spirit isn't how I would have ever imagined it, and I in no way class myself as a medium and I definitely don't have all the answers nobody does, the world is a place of endless possibilities,

Spirit for me show themselves sometimes really clear I can see the hair colour, I see the animal extremely clear, but this isn't always the case! Sometimes I have an outline or a colour that forms the shape of something but then I instantly know what it is, in the beginning add the extra 3 years I didn't know this is how I would receive, and I have probably been doing this a lot longer than I thought, I tried so many things to help me like chakra balancing, deep meditations to awaken my spiritual side when all along I was awakened I just didn't understand it and this is why I am writing this for you, because I would have really benefited from knowing what I now know then,

When I started to work with Nadine, I was so hard on myself, Nadine was amazing and still is, we now link together and see the same things, so spirit is building my confidence no end,

At first, I was so envious of people who were just so naturally getting this amazing information, it's like they weren't even trying, I felt let down I was doing everything in my power to connect, and I wouldn't change a thing because what this has done has made me appreciate any information that I get, no matter how small, of course we always want more it's only natural

Chapter 20

Channelling, meditations and more.

Channelling is when spirit use you as a host, simple as that.

Let me explain with some stories if you're like me you will understand this process a whole lot more with examples!

Circle,

We are all sitting in a circle following the teacher's guidance, when I all of a sudden feel quite faint it was as if an energy walked straight through me, I spoke up as a few had noticed I had gone quiet, and they said my whole face was changing I was

becoming a man with a moustache, I wasn't scared, more curious as I could feel my face changing, then they said it looked like I'd had a stroke! Nobody connected to this man which again left me wondering why this would happen, this happened a few times and more since I left, but now they move my body also, one of my guides had come through to tell me they had full control of my body, he wanted to show me he could use me as needed. This was comforting as now I knew he was in to totally protect me his name is White Eagle he is an Indian guide who died in 1914, he was the hereditary chief of the Ponca Indians, when White Eagle comes in he places a headdress on my head I feel it like a band around my head, but I don't always get that validation I just know he's there teaching and guiding me, another guide I work with is lord Ganesha, extremely powerful and lovely he is the overcomer of obstacles, so it

was right that I was led to him by numerous people and signs! Ganesha came in to work with us one evening and before I knew it, I was positioned like his image hands outstretched to the side I didn't even realise I was moving! So, this is how they can physically channel you and now for the talking!

I didn't even realise I was doing this but when we are talking to people giving advice sharing ideas that we don't know where they come from this is spirit giving you a helping hand, only now when I work with energies I ask them to step forward and use my voice (as I type usually as everything is online now) I just write what comes to mind and it flows beautifully, sometimes I think

is this really them or are these my thoughts but when I re-read it, I know it's come from a much higher place a place of love, no regrets, no judgement and no

negativity because that's what spirit is beautiful

energy that is love. When I have the feedback, it validates what I have given so this is always a bonus, but what I love the most is the message of how it's helped them heal, how those words have changed their grief, and that's all I ever want is to help people and all spirit want is for us to be as happy as possible in the lessons that we are learning,

What is trance mediumship?

I don't do this but have a feeling it may be on the cards for my future, it seems to be pointing in that way, Trans Is when the medium lets spirit take over their whole body, voice and mannerisms, I saw one once a gentleman and he was walking around the spirit church like an old lady talking like an old lady acting like it and I swear he didn't blink the whole time he was doing it which was over an hour! Not going to lie it freaked me out, but it doesn't now!

The images I have shared, the stories and experiences have all been encouraged by my own spirit team, here is what they say,

"we want everyone to know that when you leave this earth this is not the end of you, we are all energy we exist before life on earth, we exist on earth and we exist after, earth is a school, life is knowledge, lessons and abundance, we are born, we experience, we grow and follow paths, we are here to either learn or teach, there are so many light workers that walk this earth keeping the balance, there is not one human that has not had a spiritual experience of some sort, may it be a stranger on the platform, or a customer giving you a pound for the trolley that you forgot and have 2

screaming children hanging off you, this is all the kindness of the universe the energy of love that flows through each and every one of you here, so don't ever think that you don't have a guide or an angel, who walk every single step with you. You are love and you are loved."

Isn't spirit amazing, do I hear these words? no; do they flow through my mind and onto the keyboard yes! When I was out for a walk, they gave me an example of communicating with them, we walk the same route every day the girls love it, as we walked today, they were sniffing so much ground and were definitely picking up new scents and I remember thinking there must have been a fox here to which the reply of:

"When the humans sleep the animals play, they run here they have the freedom they deserve," So, what I'm realizing is when I've been thinking all this time and I thought common sense was answering it has in fact been spirit or our higher selves,

Here are the amazing sessions that spirit have allowed me to be a part of and grow through.

Chapter 21

My first experiences with spirit.

My first spiritual experience was years ago I remember 2 in particular one was a dream, and one was definitely not!

First was Princess Diana I was dreaming that I was brushing my teeth! And Diana appeared to the left of me she looked so sad, yet at peace she placed her hand on mine and said nothing just stared at me I stared back like we were having a silent conversation that only we understood, she left I woke up. That has always stayed with me such a beautiful visit, I was in my teens,

The next I was around 19 I had been out with friends but due to a bad chest I wasn't drinking, I got in late felt quite unwell, so went to bed lying there I felt uneasy and couldn't sleep at all, then after a while of tossing and turning, I felt a heaviness by my feet, I was absolutely terrified I opened my eyes to see if the cats had gotten in my room, but no what I saw was a young girl with blonde hair sitting on the end of my bed her head was down like she was waiting for me to speak, I knew

exactly who she was! A young girl (whose name I won't disclose as I don't have permission,)

I wasn't ready at all and actually thought I was hallucinating, I was terrified to the point I couldn't move, little girl ghosts were my biggest fear after spiders! I did speak and asked her if she was ok, but she left, she must have sensed my fear, so I know that everything I have done in my life and the way spirit have delayed my progression was for this very reason! Because now very little scares me and I'm open to absolutely anything nothing shocks me in the spirit world anymore.

Chapter 22

Pets and their messages

I have had the pleasure of doing so many sessions with these beautiful animals too many to post but here are some of the memorable ones who I have managed to get hold of for approval to be in the book.

Bailey

Bailey was a beautiful staff, who belonged to Rae,

The first thing that came to mind was the want to call the owner Rae Rae,I felt cold around my legs which was Bailey's energy, she's a very gentle cool energy and I'm being shown an older gentleman with white hair, was she put to sleep as being shown her laying on the bed and someone smoothing her head, wearing jewellery and a blouse but now I'm free are the words I have given I'm free, free from pain! not free from you they were showing me Paddy which made me think of being put to sleep this was a new way of communicating, I asked how she passed, and I felt very heavy and tired she's given a yellow rose.

Rae's response

My nickname is Rae Rae, the guy is my dad and the woman in the blouse is my mum, yes, she was put to sleep laying down in the vet I had my hand on her head doing Reiki. Two weeks before this she became ill, she had cancer and she slept a lot my legs do get cold like a breeze I just wanted to say thank you and how accurate you were.

Meet Bethoven, I was drawn to him as his mum was so sad, and there were no comments on the post, here is what happened,

Do you know why Bethoven is showing me a shark showing his teeth? Do you ever get tingles at the top of your right arm? A white light is how he's presenting himself.

DO you know the show Lassie? He is showing me a lassie dog, if you can't take it, it could be symbolic Lassie was a hero rescuing people and animals, can you take a Jack Russell with a black face? I now feel sick, so nerves anxiety does this makes sense? Carole's response. I'm not sure about the shark my husband is terrified of them even on TV he goes nuts,(VALIDATION!)tickly right arm all the time I always watched Lassie growing up, I rescue every type of animal, and my parents had a dog named Niko a mix of a Husky and collie. Chiko, my daughter's dog is that Jack Russell with a black face Rhian, this is amazing you can't imagine how happy I am to read all of this, I've tears rolling down my face as I miss him so much, but you are amazing Niko, Chiko, and most importantly my right arm I thought I was going nuts.I comment, he is happy I am literally tingling from head to toe, Carol says the anxiety must be me.

Frankie

Frankie is somewhat of a celebrity in our group, she has become extremely present in her mum's house. Here is what happened when I connected with Frankie. Frankie show's herself to me with silver on her collar as though it reflects, she's also bringing through a cat, I actually see a queen, but I feel this is more Frankie's personality, was she treated like royalty or did her personality represent royalty?

There is a dog here with black and white she is with a few animals. There is a gentleman coming in to, he has facial hair that is so neat it looks like it had been drawn on! Frankie is really happy, when she comes in she will touch the left side of your face to let you know she's near, I am picking up a quiet gentle energy with her she's not boisterous or full of energy, she's just calm and happy she showed me a memory of opening presents? there's a fatherly energy with her, she is really going to town on opening this gift, if this isn't something she loved to do then there a celebration coming up? there's so many people coming through with Frankie an older grandfather energy with white hair and a long face a little droopy, she says I'm with the people you loved! as Frankie steps back she shows me a video of her and another animal a little bigger than her and they're both looking out the back door, the other animal turns and walks away and Frankie just watches, is there another pet at home?

Carolena's response:

I am literally crying tears of happiness! This is amazing I will always hold this memory close to my heart the gentleman that came through was a friend of mine they had an incredible bond, I asked him to wait for Frankie and he really did this makes me so happy, I would always make a little goatee spell for him!!!! I believe my dad was the man with the droopiness, I have 3 more dogs at home, and they are brown this is incredible, she definitely was a queen and the matriarch of the dogs, I've had cats before Frankie, Lilo is my mum's dog that passed black and white, this is so wonderful thank you so much.

Himmie.

Himmie

Himmie, is showing me, someone hanging off the side of a bed or sofa Himmie is there being smoothed by this person, and she is loving it, but I feel she wants a treat,

I am seeing someone kneading pastry now. Halloween was mentioned,

Himmie, is showing herself sleeping behind someone s head, now I feel very lightheaded and quite faint, (Himmie, was extremely eager to talk, and this was very early on in my ac path)I'm seeing a dog do you have a dog? It is medium build with white and brown patches, there was more but these are the specifics,

Tammy's response: Rhian I was just leaning over my bed petting the other kitty in the house. She is laying in Himmies spot and has done this since her passing. I often wondered if Himmie was coming in through her. That cat was just begging for a treat!

Himmie slept behind my head often! Himmie was very ill and spaced out she had a stroke, we don't have a dog, just another cat Kitty.

Rhian my mum picked Himmies ashes up an kept them there with her for a few days she was baking pies! Himmies favourite time of year was fall and I have a Halloween ornament in the bedroom,

Tammy now has a puppy 30 weeks after this reading!

Marley

We don't have to understand messages when we are

given them, they can be very much a futuristic piece of evidence just like Tammy's beautiful cat Himmie gave her, so much healing and validation that he could see her and feel her and that she also knew what was coming for Tammy in the future.

What is a step in? it is when an energy whether

human or animal can step into a host for a limited time, just like Himmie does to Kitty and I have no doubt she does this to Marley too, they do this to feel your touch and to let you know they are there, Paddie uses Poppie and Daisey as a step in remember the picture from earlier.

I zoomed in and sent it to family members which they all replied "our best boy" that's what Paddie is our best boy so then I sent the whole phot and let's just say they were a little freaked out! I don't think they are all sceptical, but it frightens them, and things people don't understand does frighten them.

190

Jet:

When I first saw Sylvias post on Jet I couldn't help noticing, how majestic he was, so of course I wanted to try and connect to this gorgeous boy.

I'm connecting to the lovely Jet and his energy is bouncy and fun, I feel him around my lap and a huge heartbeat expressing his love for you.

He is showing me a white dog with black on his ears and head, he is thanking you for not letting him suffer, he is pain free. My legs are like jelly did he suffer with his legs?

His energy is on my right-hand tingling and my head so look out for this.

Did he love walking where there were trees? He is showing me a scene a triangle shaped tree in a picture like a Christmas scene, here comes the emotions, he is

showing me a lady in a white blouse and necklace, he Is putting his head by her chest and nuzzling her neck, real love and affection, the woman has her arm around him, and is embracing the moment.

Sylvias response:

That is very similar to the park we loved to go to, (Sylvia didn't understand who the woman was as she thought it was someone in spirit, but Jet was giving a memory and once Sylvia realised this she agreed) I would always cuddle him like this. Jet had a problem with his left back leg, he was always bouncy and full of energy, you were so right about his legs he would often stumble when we were out walking and the vet couldn't diagnose it,

I connected with Jet on another occasion also but this time it was a wow factor for me and Sylvia:

Firstly I have to say what a beautiful spirit animal he is, I feel Jet is protecting and guiding you, he really has a mystical look about him, he walks in so slowly because he wants me to see how proud and handsome he is, he showed me Father Christmas but no hat just a face and beard and the red suit, a bit like a movie Santa, the white around Jet's eyes seemed to have faded, symbolic so he's younger now and there's a young energy about him, he's coming through quite confidently and I see a man's face but not clearly as yet. You will feel a tingle on your lip and paw on the left side of your face! My door just knocked three times!!! it frightened the life out of me!!

I'm in my converted garage and the door is in my garden and there is no one there so I'm getting three is significant so look out for three things, or something happening three times. (Then, I was brought to the attention of the name jet J.E.T.3 letters that's him I was covered in my confirmation goosepimples. I'm seeing a grandmother energy

with the biggest Angel wings watching over you.
Now there are toys going off and it has absolutely
frightened the life out of me! do you have things
like this happening with you they're trying to get
your attention; the funny thing was the toy that
went off was a Doc Mcstuffins and the words were
"let me help you" I won't lie I thought I might have
a slight heart attack! I'm seeing an old man and
he's kindly taken out his teeth out! there's so much
protection around you I feel the breeze it in front
of me now, and this energy is coming up so close,
but it is protective! do you ever feel it?

Spirit is so funny they're probably trying to calm
my heart down because they know I don't like
seeing people without teeth in! Jet is also bringing
in laughter for you, now I'm seeing a jester! spirit
want you laughing more Jet loved to see you
laugh, I feel pressure on my heart now and again
like a paw so when you laugh it makes his heart
happy! did he make you laugh a lot?

I'm seeing a Man's face an impression of a stage
like going to theatres or show now I see a cow
with its tongue hanging out and it's going back

and forth like o'clock the actual tongue. Now I'm being given a man sitting down, playing an accordion, he's very laidback and has a calm manner. I Have a lady in a light coat a gentleman in a dark coat that are still living, the ladies locking the front door and off they go for a walk, and I feel Jet is showing me this as he walks with you still. The person with the accordion is there with Jet smoothing him standing by his side please know they are saying he is safe with family! who had a collar and it sparkled?

Long isn't it, and wow jam packed I was praying Sylvia could relate to, well any of it. This was one of the sessions that had my heart racing, spirit was letting me know what is possible and how energy can do pretty much anything.

Sylvias response:

just a short while ago I felt pressure like something touching my chin, and as I write this, I feel it again this makes me happy. I was told not long ago that my grandmother is my guardian Angel and this afternoon I heard a clicking noise coming from the area where his toy box was. I don't know who the

man with the false teeth is, but it made me laugh.
(spirit will do this to lighten the session) I often feel
as though I'm outside even when I'm inside and it's
warm sometimes I get a feather like feel of cold a
particular on my feet.(this is energy coming
around Sylvia letting her know they're there,) The
man in the theatre could very well be my uncle, As
for the cows, on Jet's last day at the vets we had
to wait at the side of the surgery and all the cows
in the field came over to Jet he had never seen
them before and it scared him, (I reply they don't
scare him anymore they looked really silly) Oh my
God my dad used to play the accordion that is my
dad! you'll soon have met my entire family! We
had a snow marbled Bengal that had a pink
sparkly collar I am sorry jet scared you by knocking
the door ha-ha I can't express enough how
grateful for the help you gave me!

By the way last night, me and my husband went
for a walk I locked the front door I wore a white
jumper and my husband a black coat!

It doesn't matter how little you think the message is, it could mean the absolute world to someone else!

I once had a session not so great session, a dog let's call her Pixie, the first thing I heard was shower, the mum burst into tears and said oh my god! I showered her the night before she died and felt so bad does she forgive me, I replied spirit only bring things up for you to know there's no regrets, she is thanking you, after that everything went downhill she couldn't take anything, I saw the dog with huge teats and asked if she was rescued no said the owner, then she sent me pictures later on of the dogs daughter and grandchildren so the dog had numerus pups, never assume always give what you see like catchphrase, if I had said why is she showing me enlarged teats then that would have led to more validation!

Working spiritually is not easy, there is so much trust, concentration and understanding involved, so to be where I am today and see all these people that I have, is a true blessing for me and I will never ever take this for granted!

Bonny

Meet Bonny, this was Sylvias first dog and as I was writing about Jet Bonny's name kept popping in, Bonny would like to part of the book too!

Here is Bonny's session.

Did Bonnie struggle with her legs? mine have gone really heavy! I'm sitting here quietly, eyes close connected into your beautiful girl when all of a sudden my dog from nowhere jumps up and kisses me on my face, and I swear she's picking up on the spirit did Bonnie ever do this? feels the tingles up your left arm she is so relaxed and calm such a peaceful energy coming off her, tingling all over my head now, she's getting stronger I'm asking for confirmation field ask her to please send memories maybe talk to about to memory you have,

she showed me the brightest white light and a elephant which is my symbol for I'll ever get you she showing me now sitting and her 2 front paws begging, my whole head is tingling can you feel it I been shown a younger dog black and brown they had the collar with a shiny disc on it, and they are kissing you all over the face the affection and love I'm seeing is just unbelievable, please know the love from your Bonny and Jet I feel is coming back to you.

Sylvias response:

at the end Bonnie couldn't stand on her back legs she slipped on ice and we thought you'd broken some bones the vet couldn't help her she was 15 1/2 years old when she passed away she was a very affectionate dog I could never forget I can't thank you enough for everything you do Bonnie was so special bursting with energy but so calm and patient with children the begging was her way of telling us to carry on making a fuss of her, Jet would do the same only more insistent, we're at the moment on a puppy list the same breed as Bonny and Jet! Beautiful and Bonny is still very active as I write this the same feeling buzzing around my head such a beautiful energy.

Captain Hastings:

Captain Hastings was this beautiful golden brown, bundle of charm. I could not resist but to connect to him so as I did he said, "no more tears" he tickles my right ear like he's sniffing, my dogs do this and I call it whispers, so look out for that and

now he shows me what Poppie does when she's begging for a treat with the two paws, he's singing history now by One Direction and saying "we were the greatest team" I asked him what did he love to do and he shows me a sofa and a remote control for the TV, this made me laugh, have you lost the remote recently as he shows me you laying on the sofa and at first it looked like you were swimming but now I think you are in search of the remote control, not wanting to get up. He's with a man who might have liked to paint like a dad or granddad energy, can you understand stomach pains or stomach cramps, and now I'm seeing someone with a huge book, as if they are opening a piano book or knitting pattern that about to do something but I cannot see it clearly enough, so it is piano or sewing machine maybe. He's so beautiful like a Prince valiant that's what I want to call him please take his love he loves you all the stars and more I hope some of this resonates and brings healing.

Ines response:

Dear Rhian, I will answer you shortly I must recollect myself but this first you are a wonderful person. Rhian you will never know what you're reading did for me I was crying so hard like I had done the day my boy went to the other side. The wound in my heart felt so fresh and my heartbeat accelerated. But this way I knew your messages we're truly from Hastings. Yes, I was crying a lot since I've lost him every day, and yes, he would bite my right ear every time I came home, this was simply his habit since he was a puppy, and it can actually have a second meaning since it is a new puppy of mine and he also began to bite my ear 4 weeks ago and has done this ever since. Yes, he did the begging, and he did this all the time in the way your Poppie does.

He was singing to you oh my gosh, I used to sing to him when we were driving in the car the meaning of that song is so much more "so don't let it go, we can make some more, we can live forever" we were the greatest team, yes, we were, and we still are and maybe he is coming back to me. He loved to go on the sofa in the evening and snuggle up against me and yes looking for the TV remote, we were searching for that all the time, but I did not dare to disturb him sleeping. The man you saw could be my father I am so happy to hear they are together, I lost him to lung cancer, and he could actually play the piano very well, stomach pains and cramps Hastings was diagnosed with lymphoma, he was often suffering from those pains after chemotherapy my poor boy! Piano, sewing machine I was visiting a good friend of mine for Christmas to bring her a gift she was showing me her new work a really huge wool blanket and there's more after a critical surgery Hastings was going through because of his cancer he nearly died I was praying so hard I made a pledge to God that if he would save him I would give my best friends a good sum of money she told me now at that very Christmas that she has bought a sewing machine from the sum,

Rhian, I was just writing to a friend to tell her about your amazing reading, and I re-read your messages I was struggling for the right word for "PRINZ EISENHERZ" because I was remembering I would call Hastings this in the last month often I thought it would be somewhat like iron heart, but the correct translation would come up and it was Prince valiant! I am totally stunned again your reading was indeed a one of a kind thank you. The story of Hastings did not end there after going through a few readings in the group Hastings has popped up in quite a few messages before he was even a member of the group. He has become quite a celebrity in the animal communication world. I connected with Hastings again, but he had so much to say I would have to make a new book!

Chapter 23

More validations.

Some animals came through before my animal communication started, Paddie brought them through so I could tell their mums they were ok here are a few of their images.

Lilly the boy passed a week after Paddie, my mums' cat.

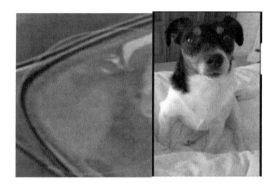

Twinkle my cousins' dog is a regular visitor with Paddie.

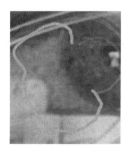

This happy chap was a friend of a friends, dog he was bouncing in his name was Dexter. I could see Paddie by his side,

This was Narla, my friends American bulldog, I was sending healing as she transitioned, and this is what she sent me.

This was so clear to everyone; we were at Disney on ice and the camera caught my gran and if you look closely you will see my Grampa there too.

My gran is permanently on my living room wall accompanied with a lioness.

I understand that not everyone will see these energies in my pictures, and that is fine, we are all on this journey at our own pace and here to fulfil our purpose, whatever your belief is or whatever it is your drawn to as long as you believe in yourself you can do anything. I believe in you!

Thank you for reading my book if you got to the end well done.

"When you are searching for yourself, remember to start from within, only then will you find what you are looking for."

"Oh, my life is changing every day,

In every possible way,

and oh, my dreams

it's never quite as it seems,

never quite as it seems"

(The Cranberries)

"I think of what, the world

Could be, a vision of the one I see,

A million dreams are keeping

Me awake"

(The Greatest showman)

"Even if you cannot hear my voice

I am right beside you dear"

(Run Leona Lewis)

AKNOWLEDGMENTS

With thanks to all the pet parents and their beautiful animals who have made my dream become a reality:

- *Carolena Hollifield and the beautiful Frankie.*

- *Melissa Doyle the beautiful Gracie and the hilarious Frank.*

- *Carole Lapensee and the Handsome Bethoven.*

- *Rae Halpert and the elegant Bailey.*

- *Carrie Purcel and the beautiful Lexi.*

- *Flossie Balchunis O'donnell and the gorgeous Holly and Puppy.*

- *Kat Lee and Mr handsome pants himself Coby.*

- *Lisa Lishman and the elegant Ruby.*

- *Sylvia Hursthouse and the majestic Jet and Bonny.*

- *Candice Boney and the wise and handsome Colby and Obbie the teacher.*

- *Ines Windhoefer and Prince Valiant that is Hastings.*

And for the photo graphic evidence of the pet visitors, and also for allowing me to mention our experiences in my book.

- *Trudi Portingale and the gorgeous star that is Twinkle.*

- *Cerys Phillips and beautiful handsome boy Lilly.*

- *Hayley Shellard.*

- *Audrey Mcnaughton*

Thank you, Karen Anderson and your book,

> *"The amazing afterlife of animals," Your book changed my world as it did many others, I thank you for all the opportunities and support you have given me over the past year. You are a true gift to the animal kingdom and the world.*

Thank you, to Nadine Phillips a special lady who I am honoured, to work Alongside, You, are the reason I now understand who I am, keep shining your beautiful light.

Jane Fishlock, thank you, for the endless video chats, helping me, healing me, guiding, and uplifting me. You are a remarkable Lady who I am so privileged to know!

Lisa O'sullivan Thomas, thank you, for having all the "patience "With me, even though I would make you scream! You are a true light in the world.

Thank you to my parents:

My mum Cerys, who has a heart of pure gold and the encouragement of a million fans, you always support me in whatever I choose so, thank you for being the parent I needed,

> *And my dad, Mark, this freaks you out, and you pretend you don't hear it, but I know you do I have my spies! Thank you for being you dad, thank you for saying yes eventually to all the animals! You are a different version of Dr Dolittle yourself.*

Thank you to my grandparents for instilling wisdom, respect, and the hundreds of stories of the world you lived in.

Most importantly, my family my children, and my husband Andrew, you have all supported everything I do, and this I thought would have pushed you out of your comfort zone, but you let me find out who I am, and I will always be grateful for that. Thank you to you all for being mine.

And thank you for reading this book, I truly hope it has helped you, to embrace the beautiful person you are.

Now go out into the world believe in yourself and do what makes your heart smile!

And finally, I have to say writing this book has been the most awakening experience ever! Reliving my journey I can see now how everything had to happen exactly as it did, trust in your journey, nothing is wasted everything will fit in and have a place or teach you a lesson, remember it, thank it and most importantly don't dismiss the importance of patience, it really is worth it when you finally find your purpose.

"One step, one breath, one day, you will get where you need to be, remember, it's not how quick you get there, it's what you learn that is what's important."

Conclusion, I am still very early on in my growth and development, I have so much more to learn and experience, this is just where I am now and I'm hoping this has inspired you to keep fighting the frustrations and follow your dreams, I know I have plenty more to frustrations, patience and eye rolling's to come, there are so many talented people out there I am just so relieved I have finally been allowed into this world!

" In the silence we grow"

Rhian clark

Printed in Great Britain
by Amazon

63873475R00124